The Hampstead Clinic Psychoanalytic Library
(Concept Research Group)

VOLUME III
BASIC PSYCHOANALYTIC CONCEPTS
ON THE THEORY OF INSTINCTS

In the same series

Ed. Dr Humberto Nagera

BASIC PSYCHOANALYTIC CONCEPTS ON THE THEORY OF INSTINCTS

by
HUMBERTO NAGERA

and
S. BAKER, R. EDGCUMBE, A. HOLDER
M. LAUFER, D. MEERS, K. REES

BASIC BOOKS, INC., PUBLISHERS

NEW YORK

© 1970 by George Allen and Unwin, Ltd.
Library of Congress Catalog Card Number: 71-152786
SBN 465-00575-6
Printed in the United States of America

ACKNOWLEDGEMENTS AND COPYRIGHT NOTICES

The editor and publishers wish to thank the following publishers for their kind permission to use the material noted:

The Hogarth Press and the London Institute of Psychoanalysis for permission to quote from all volumes of the Standard Edition of the *Complete Psychological Works of Sigmund Freud.*

Routledge & Kegan Paul Ltd. for permission to quote from the following publications of Freud:
Jokes and their Relation to the Unconscious
Totem and Taboo
Leonardo da Vinci and a Memory of his Childhood

W. W. Norton for permission to quote from the following publications of Freud:

The Claims of Psychoanalysis to Scientific Interest
Jokes and their Relation to the Unconscious
Civilization and its Discontents
The Ego and the Id
Leonardo da Vinci and a Memory of his Childhood
The Question of Lay Analysis
Totem and Taboo
Inhibitions, Symptoms and Anxiety
New Introductory Lectures on Psycho-Analysis

Liveright for permission to quote from the following publications of Freud:

Beyond the Pleasure Principle
Introductory Lectures on Psycho-Analysis
Five Lectures on Psycho-Analysis

Thanks are due to the Sigmund Freud Copyrights for their permission and generous co-operation.

FOREWORD TO
THE HAMPSTEAD CLINIC LIBRARY

The series of publications of which the present volume forms a part, will be welcomed by all those readers who are concerned with the history of psychoanalytic concepts and interested to follow the vicissitudes of their fate through the theoretical, clinical and technical writings of psychoanalytic authors. On the one hand, these fates may strike us as being very different from each other. On the other hand, it proves not too difficult to single out some common trends and to explore the reasons for them.

There are some terms and concepts which served an important function for psychoanalysis in its earliest years because of their being simple and all-embracing such as for example the notion of a 'complex'. Even the lay public understood more or less easily that what was meant thereby was any cluster of impulses, emotions, thoughts, etc. which have their roots in the unconscious and, exerting their influence from there, give rise to anxiety, defences and symptom formation in the conscious mind. Accordingly, the term was used widely as a form of psychological short-hand. 'Father-Complex', 'Mother-Complex', 'Guilt-Complex', 'Inferiority-Complex', etc. became familiar notions. Nevertheless, in due course, added psychoanalytical findings about the child's relationship to his parents, about the early mother-infant tie and its consequences, about the complexities of lacking self-esteem and feelings of insufficiency and inferiority demanded more precise conceptualization. The very omnibus nature of the term could not but lead to its, at least partial, abandonment. All that remained from it were the terms 'Oedipus Complex' to designate the experiences centred around the triangular relationships of the phallic phase, and 'Castration-Complex' for the anxieties, repressed wishes, etc. concerning the loss or lack of the male sexual organ.

If, in the former instance, a general concept was split up to make room for more specific meanings, in other instances concepts took turns in the opposite direction. After starting out as concrete, well-defined descriptions of circumscribed psychic events, they were applied by many authors to an ever-widening circle of phenomena until their connotation became increasingly vague and imprecise and until finally special efforts had to be made to re-define them, to restrict their sphere of application and to invest them once more with precision and significance. This is what happened, for example, to the concepts of *Transference* and of *Trauma*.

The concept and term 'transference' was designed originally to establish the fact that the realistic relationship between analyst and patient is invariably distorted by phantasies and object-relations which stem from the patient's past and that these very distortions can be turned into a technical tool to reveal the patient's past pathogenic history. In present days, the meaning of the term has been widened to the extent that it comprises whatever happens between analyst and patient regardless of its derivation and of the reasons for its happening.

A 'trauma' or 'traumatic happening' meant originally an (external or internal) event of a magnitude with which the individual's ego is unable to deal, i.e. a sudden influx of excitation, massive enough to break through the ego's normal stimulus barrier. To this purely quantitative meaning of the term were added in time all sorts of qualifications (such as cumulative, retrospective, silent, beneficial), until the concept ended up as more or less synonymous with the notion of a pathogenic event in general.

Psychoanalytic concepts may be overtaken also by a further fate, which is perhaps of even greater significance. Most of them owe their origin to a particular era of psychoanalytic theory, or to a particular field of clinical application, or to a particular mode of technique. Since any of the backgrounds in which they are rooted, are open to change, this should lead either to a corresponding change in the concepts or to their abandonment. But, most frequently, this has failed to happen. Many concepts are carried forward through the changing scene of psychoanalytic theory and practice without sufficient thought being given to their necessary alteration or re-definition.

A case in kind is the concept of *acting out*. It was created at the very outset of technical thinking and teaching, tied to the treatment of neurotic patients, and it characterized originally a specific reaction of these patients to the psychoanalytic technique, namely that certain items of their past, when retrieved from the unconscious, did not return to conscious memory but revealed themselves instead in behaviour, were 'acted on', or 'acted out' instead of being remembered. By now, this clear distinction between remembering the recovered past and re-living it has been obscured;

the term 'acting out' is used out of this context, notably for patients such as adolescents, delinquents or psychotics whose impulse-ridden behaviour is part of their original pathology and not the direct consequence of analytic work done on the ego's defences against the repressed unconscious.

It was in this state of affairs that Dr H. Nagera initiated his enquiry into the history of psychoanalytic thinking. Assisted by a team of analytic workers, trained in the Hampstead Child-Therapy Course and Clinic, he set out to trace the course of basic psycho-analytic concepts from their first appearance through their changes in the twenty-three volumes of the *Standard Edition* of *The Complete Psychological Works of Sigmund Freud*, i.e. to a point from where they are meant to be taken further to include the writings of the most important authors of the post-Freudian era.

Dr Nagera's aim in this venture was a fourfold one:

to facilitate for readers of psychoanalytic literature the understanding of psychoanalytic thought and of the terminology in which it is expressed;

to understand and define concepts, not only according to their individual significance, but also according to their relevance for the particular historical phase of psychoanalytic theory within which they have arisen;

to induce psychoanalytic authors to use their terms and concepts more precisely with regard for the theoretical framework to which they owe their origin, and to reduce thereby the many sources of misunderstanding and confusion which govern the psychoanalytic literature at present;

finally, to create for students of psychoanalysis the opportunity to embark on a course of independent reading and study, linked to a scholarly aim and designed to promote their critical and constructive thinking on matters of theory-formation.

Anna Freud, London

CONTENTS

INTRODUCTION

This volume is a sample of scholastic research work carried out at the Hampstead Child Therapy Clinic and Course relating to the study of a large number of pre-selected psychoanalytic concepts postulated and developed by Freud in his psychoanalytic writings, spanning the time from his earliest to his latest conceptualizations.

This research work has been carried out during the last six years by the Concept Research Group. These drafts on basic concepts are in no way meant to replace the study of Freud's works themselves. On the contrary, they are intended as a guide to help the student in that very aim.

The group's method has been to assign to each of its members one pre-selected concept at a time. This member's task then is to extract all the relevant material from Freud's published papers, books, correspondence, Minutes of the Meetings of the Vienna Psychoanalytic Society, etc., and to prepare a written summary of a given concept for discussion. This first draft is referred to as the 'personal draft' and is circulated among members some time before it is due for discussion.

As far as possible the draft makes use of 'literal quotations', giving at the same time the source of the quotations. This facilitates the study of the drafts by the group members who meet weekly to discuss the personal drafts. On the basis of the general discussion by the Group a second draft is produced which we designate as the 'group draft'.

Our aims are multiple and are very much in accordance with the views expressed by Hartmann, Kris and Loewenstein in their paper 'The Function of Theory in Psychoanalysis'[1] and in other publications.

Like these authors, we believe that Freud's views are often misrepresented in a considerable number of the vast amount of psychoanalytic writings due to the fact that certain of Freud's statements are not always evaluated within their proper context.

[1] Hartmann, H., Kris, E., Loewenstein, R. M., 'The Function of Theory in Psychoanalysis', *Drives, Affects and Behaviour*, International Universities Press, Inc., New York, 1953.

Thus, not infrequently, specific aspects are torn out of a long historical line of theoretical development and isolated from the rest, and similarly one or the other phase of psychoanalytic thinking is given undue emphasis out of context. Such misrepresentations are apt to convey the erroneous impression that whatever aspect has been singled out embraces all that Freud or psychoanalysis had ever to say on some specific topic. In this sense we very much endorse the statement made by Hartmann, Kris and Loewenstein that 'quoting Freud is, as a rule, meaningful only if it is part of a laborious but unavoidable attempt to gain insight into the position of the quoted passage within the development of Freud's thought'.[1] This is precisely one of the major aims of the Concept Research Group.

We were similarly prompted for what we felt with Hartmann, Kris and Loewenstein, to be 'the disregard for the psychoanalytic theory as a coherent set of assumptions'.[2] 'Freud's hypotheses are interrelated in a systematic way: there is a hierarchy of hypothesis in their relevance, their closeness to observation, their degree of verification. It is none the less true that there exists no comprehensive presentation of analysis from this angle. Here again recourse to the historical approach seems imperative . . . by showing the actual problems in their right proportions and in their right perspective.'[3]

Another important factor is the realization that Freud made many statements in the course of developing his theories which he withdrew or modified in subsequent works. This in itself constitutes a major source of frequent misrepresentation of Freud's views. One of the aims of this work, in which we try to evaluate Freud's basic psychoanalytic concepts in their historical context, is precisely to avoid such pitfalls and misrepresentations.

We further agree with Hartmann, Kris and Loewenstein that a serious danger of misrepresentation exists when there is an insufficient understanding of the hierarchy of psychoanalytic propositions. It is therefore essential to have a clear understanding of

[1] Hartmann, H., 'The Development of the Ego Concept in Freud's Work', I.J.P., Vol. XXXVII, Part VI, 1956. (Paper read at the Freud Centenary Meeting of the British Psycho-Analytical Society, May 5, 1956.)

[2] Hartmann, H., Kris, E., Loewenstein, R. M., 'The Function of Theory in Psychoanalysis', *Drives, Affects and Behaviour*, International Universities Press, Inc., New York, 1953, p. 23.

[3] Hartmann, H., 'The Development of the Ego Concept in Freud's Work', *International Journal of Psychonalysis*, Vol. XXXVII, Part VI, 1956, p. 425.

how the different parts of psychoanalytic theoretical propositions fit together, both when quoting and when attempting new formulations.

We are planning to publish the remainder of the work of the Concept Research Group up to the present moment in the near future in order to make it available to teachers and students in the psychoanalytic and related fields. We think that this contribution will be of special value and interest to any student of Freud, especially students in training who will have an encyclopaedic review of basic psychoanalytic concepts in an extremely condensed but meaningful way. From these summaries of concepts the student can readily find his way back to Freud's work in order to pursue and become more fully acquainted with his formulations. In this way he can study specific aspects in the development of the theory while being able, at the same time, to get a more comprehensive and over-all view of the particular topic and its relations with other aspects of the theory. We believe that our work will be similarly useful to lecturers and seminar leaders, to research workers in the field of psychoanalysis and related fields and to those writing papers which require a review of Freud's statements with regard to a specific topic. Altogether this form of scholastic research may help to avoid confusion, constant reformulations and the introduction of new terms when authors in fact refer to 'concepts' already clearly described by Freud in the past. This work may well help to open the way to standardize and find some measure of agreement as to the precise meaning of terms used in psychoanalysis today.

Although we have taken as much care as possible to be comprehensive and to avoid misrepresentations, experience has taught us that we can have no claim to perfection or completeness. It is practically impossible, within a vast and complex volume of theory such as Freud's life output represents, not to overlook or even slightly to misrepresent one or another aspect or set of factors. Furthermore, the capacity to comprehend and the level of insight possible for any given person or group of persons engaged in such work increases as the work proceeds. Thus certain formulations become more meaningful, are suddenly understood in a new light, assume a different significance, etc. Because of our realization of potential shortcomings we hope that future readers of these concepts will contribute to complete and clarify the work which the Concept Group has started, by drawing our attention to relevant material which has been either overlooked, misrepresented or not understood in its full significance.

It is hoped that in this way the concepts will become more and more representative and complete in the course of time.

Dr Humberto Nagera

INSTINCT AND DRIVE

In the original German of Freud's works the terms '*Instinkt*' or '*instinktiv*' appear in five works only, namely in *Totem and Taboo* (1912–13), in the paper on 'The Unconscious' (1915e), in the clinical paper 'From the History of an Infantile Neurosis' (1918b [1914]), in *Group Psychology and the Analysis of the Ego* (1921c) and in *Inhibitions, Symptoms and Anxiety* (1926d). In his descriptions of instinctual urges, impulsions, needs, or drives, Freud invariably used the term '*Trieb*'. In the *Standard Edition* Freud's term '*Trieb*' has been translated by 'instinct' throughout. It is important to bear this in mind, as Freud makes a clear distinction between '*Instinkt*' and '*Trieb*'.

In the General Preface to the *Standard Edition* the editors argue that 'from the standpoint of modern biology, Freud used the word "*Trieb*" to cover a variety of different concepts'. For this reason they rejected the suggestion of rendering Freud's '*Trieb*' by 'drive' and gave preference to choosing 'an obviously vague and indeterminate word' like 'instinct'.[1]

Jones, in his biography of Freud, points out that '. . . the German word *Trieb* is less committal than the English "instinct", which definitely implies an inborn and inherited character.

'Other words such as "urge", "impulsion" or the more colloquial and expressive American "drive", have been suggested as translations, but none of them is entirely satisfactory. On the whole the word in Freud's writings more often means "instinct" in our sense.'[2]

In four of the passages where Freud uses the term '*Instinkt*' with regard to human beings he makes the comparison with phenomena as they can be observed in the animal world. But whereas there can be no doubt about the existence of *Triebe* in every human being, Freud is more doubtful as to the existence of *Instinkte* in human beings: 'If inherited mental formations exist in the human being—something analogous to instinct [*Instinkt*] in

[1] Editor's General Preface, S.E., Vol. 1, p. 25.
[2] Jones, E., *Sigmund Freud. Life and Work*, The Hogarth Press, London 1958, Vol. 2, p. 354.

animals—these constitute the nucleus of the *Ucs*.[1] This seems to point to a first important differentiation between an *Instinkt* and a *Trieb* in Freud's view. Whilst *Instinkte* are 'inherited mental formations', a *Trieb* is a frontier-concept 'between the mental and the physical', and the 'source of an instinct [*Trieb*] is a process of excitation occurring in an organ',[2] which subsequently may find a —conscious or unconscious—representation.[3] In the continuation of the above quotation from 'The Unconscious' Freud maintains a clear distinction between the two: 'Later there is added to them [*den Instinkten*] what is discarded during childhood development as unserviceable; and this need not differ in its nature from what is inherited. A sharp and final division between the content of the two systems does not, as a rule, take place till puberty'[4] (The meaning of the last sentence seems somewhat obscure.)

Other passages seem to suggest that when Freud is talking of *Instinkte* he is not so much talking of them in regard to internal phenomena but of an inherited recognition of external situations, particularly danger situations:

'The external (real) danger must also have managed to become internalized if it is to be significant for the ego. It must have been recognized as related to some situation of helplessness that has been experienced. Man seems not to have been endowed, or to have been endowed to only a very small degree, with an instinctive [*instinktiv*] recognition of the dangers that threaten him from without. Small children are constantly doing things which endanger their lives, and that is precisely why they cannot afford to be without a protecting object. In relation to the traumatic situation, in which the subject is helpless, external and internal dangers, real dangers and instinctual demands [*Triebanspruch*] converge ... the fear of small animals, thunderstorms, etc., might perhaps be accounted for as vestigial traces of the congenital preparedness to meet real dangers which is so strongly developed in other animals.'[5]

In discussing the later reactivation of the primal scene observation made by the Wolf Man at the age of one-and-a-half, Freud makes a similar point:

[1] (1915e) 'The Unconscious', S.E., Vol. 14, p. 195.
[2] (1905d [1915]), *Three Essays on the Theory of Sexuality*, S.E., Vol. 7, p. 168.
[3] (1915e) 'The Unconscious', S.E., Vol. 14. p. 177.   [4] ibid., p. 195.
[5] (1926d) *Inhibitions, Symptoms and Anxiety*, S.E. Vol., 20, p. 168.

'It is hard to dismiss the view that some sort of hardly definable knowledge, something, as it were, preparatory to an understanding, was at work in the child at the time. We can form no conception of what this may have consisted in; we have nothing at our disposal but the single analogy—and it is an excellent one—of the far-reaching *instinctive* [*instinktiv*] knowledge of animals.

If human beings, too, possessed an instinctive [*instinktiv*] endowment such as this, it would not be surprising that it should be very particularly concerned with the processes of sexual life, even though it could not be by any means confined to them. This instinctive [*instinktiv*] factor would then be the nucleus of the unconscious, a primitive kind of mental activity, which would later be dethroned and overlaid by human reason, when that faculty came to be acquired, but which in some people, perhaps in everyone, would retain the power of drawing down to it the higher mental processes.'[1]

Implicit in the last sentence of this passage seems to be a further distinction between an *Instinkt* and a *Trieb*. Whereas a *Trieb* is defined by Freud as 'an endosomatic, continuously flowing source of stimulation' and is regarded as 'a measure of the demand made upon the mind for work' with the 'immediate aim of . . . the removal of this organic stimulus',[2] an *Instinkt*, in Freud's sense, does not seem to have the qualities of a continuous internal stimulation, of making demands on the mind, and its aim seems to lie more in self-preservation than in the removal of an organic stimulus. Furthermore, the vicissitudes of *Triebe*, described by Freud in 'Instincts and their Vicissitudes' ('*Triebe und Triebschicksale*'), do not seem to apply to the inherited mental formations called '*Instinkte*' by Freud.

These considerations lead us to a last difference inherent in Freud's distinction between *Instinkten* and *Trieben*. One of the characteristics of the latter is that they continuously seek discharge or satisfaction. This does not seem to apply in the case of an *Instinkt*.

In the remaining two works (*Totem and Taboo* and *Group Psychology*) Freud uses the term '*Instinkt*' in reviewing some literature relevant to the respective topics discussed, but neither passage throws any further light on the precise meaning which the concept of *Instinkt* had for Freud.

[1] (1918b [1914]) 'From the History of an Infantile Neurosis', S.E., Vol. 17, p. 120.
[2] (1905d [1915]) *Three Essays on the Theory of Sexuality*, S.E., Vol. 7, p. 168.

In *Totem and Taboo* Freud discusses and discards Westermarck's contention that the 'horror of incest' should be regarded as a consequence of an innate instinct (*Instinkt*).

'A biological instinct [*Instinkt*] of the kind suggested would scarcely have gone so far astray in its psychological expression that, instead of applying to blood relatives (intercourse with whom might be injurious to reproduction), it affected persons who were totally innocuous in this respect, merely because they shared a common home. . . . Thus the view which explains the horror of incest as an innate instinct [*Instinkt*] must be abandoned.'[1]

In *Group Psychology* the term '*Instinkt*' appears several times in the context of Freud's discussion of Trotter's work on *Instincts of the Herd in Peace and War* (1916). Freud does not seem to make a clear distinction between *Trieb* and *Instinkt*, using the term '*Herdeninstinkt*' in one paragraph, '*Herdentrieb*' in another.[2]

We should like to add two other passages which may help to throw some light on Freud's use of the terms '*Instinkt*' and '*Trieb*'. The first one seems to indicate that he uses the term '*Trieb*' to denote something which differs from the more commonly used '*Instinkt*': 'We give these bodily needs, in so far as they represent an instigation to mental activity, the name of "*Triebe*" [instincts] a word for which we are envied by many modern languages.'[3]

On the other hand, in his Preface to Reik's *Ritual: Psycho-analytic Studies* (1919) we read the following sentence: 'These instincts [*Triebe*] which have fallen victim to repression—untamed and indestructible, yet inhibited from any kind of activity—together with their primitive mental representatives, constitute the mental underworld, the nucleus of the true unconscious, and are at every moment ready to assert their demands and, by hook or by crook, to force their way forward to satisfaction.'[4] In the characteristic of forming the 'nucleus of the true unconscious' this definition of '*Triebe*' comes close to that given by Freud of '*Instinkte*' in his paper on 'The Unconscious'.[5]

[1] (1912–13) *Totem and Taboo*, S.E., Vol. 13, p. 123n.

[2] (1921c) *Group Psychology and the Analysis of the Ego*, S.E., Vol. 18, pp. 117–20.

[3] (1926c) *The Question of Lay Analysis*, S.E., Vol. 20, p. 200.

[4] (1919g) Preface to Reik's *Ritual: Psychoanalytic Studies*, S.E., Vol. 17, p. 260.

[5] See reference 1 on p. 20 above.

THE DEVELOPMENT OF FREUD'S INSTINCT THEORY, 1894–1939

I. INTRODUCTION AND DEFINITION

Freud's efforts to understand the nature of the forces participating in mental conflict arose out of his clinical experience with neurotic, and later psychotic patients (see Concept: Conflict). The development of his clinical understanding, and of the theoretical postulates by means of which he sought to order and explain normal and pathological processes in mental life, are therefore determined by the clinical material available to him at any given time. He sought to construct theoretical models of the mind, the mental apparatus, and the processes operating within it, and to distinguish and order the internal and external stimuli which impinge upon the mental apparatus, setting its processes in motion. By far the most important of these stimuli are the instincts.

Freud's definition of instincts approached the subject from two aspects: their nature and composition, and their effects upon the mental apparatus, e.g.:

'By an "instinct" is provisionally to be understood the psychical representative of an endosomatic, continuously flowing source of stimulation, as contrasted with a "stimulus", which is set up by *single* excitations coming from *without*. The concept of instinct is thus one of those lying on the frontier between the mental and the physical. The simplest and likeliest assumption as to the nature of instincts would seem to be that in itself an instinct is without quality, and, so far as mental life in concerned, is only to be regarded as a measure of the demand made upon the mind for work. What distinguishes the instincts from one another and endows them with specific qualities is their relation to their somatic sources and to their aims. The source of an instinct is a process of excitation occurring in an organ and the immediate aim of the instinct lies in the removal of this organic stimulus.'[1]

Elsewhere he distinguishes more sharply between instincts and their ideational representatives:

[1] (1905d [1915]) *Three Essays on the Theory of Sexuality*, S.E., Vol. 7, p. 168.

23

'I am in fact of the opinion that the antithesis of conscious and unconscious is not applicable to instincts. An instinct can never become an object of consciousness—only the idea that represents the instinct can. Even in the unconscious, moreover, an instinct cannot be represented otherwise than by an idea. If the instinct did not attach itself to an idea or manifest itself as an affective state, we could know nothing about it. When we nevertheless speak of an unconscious instinctual impulse or of a repressed instinctual impulse, the looseness of phraseology is a harmless one. We can only mean an instinctual impulse the ideational representative of which is unconscious, for nothing else comes into consideration.'[1]

II. THE BIOLOGICAL AND PSYCHOLOGICAL CONCEPTS OF INSTINCT

Once Freud had moved away from his early neurological orientation he gave up attempts to describe psychical phenomena in terms of physical events, and tried to evolve a purely psychological theory. But the sphere of instincts was the most difficult area in which to separate the psychological from the biological as is shown in the definitions Freud gave. However, Freud stated many times that psychoanalysis was concerned only with the mental aspects of instinctual life, e.g.:

'Instincts and their transformations are at the limit of what is discernable by psycho-analysis. From that point it gives place to biological research.'[2]
'Psycho-analysts never forget that the mental is based on the organic, although their work can only carry them as far as this basis and not beyond it.'[3]

Further, as can be seen from the second definition given in the introduction,[4] after 1915 Freud made it clear that only the ideational representatives of instincts are possible subjects for psycho-

[1] (1915e) 'The Unconscious', S.E., Vol. 14, p. 177.
[2] (1910c) *Leonardo da Vinci and a Memory of his Childhood*, S.E., Vol. 11, p. 136.
[3] (1910i) 'The Psycho-Analytic View of Psychogenic Disturbances of Vision', S.E., Vol. 11, p. 217.
[4] (1915e) 'The Unconscious', S.E., Vol. 14, p. 177.

analytic consideration. Without such representation we could know nothing of the drives themselves.

For many years Freud adhered to his decision to deal only with the psychical aspects of instincts. But eventually he found himself obliged to plunge into biological theory once again, in the postulation of the life and death instincts.

'Though psycho-analysis endeavours as a rule to develop its theories as independently as possible from those of other sciences, it is nevertheless obliged to seek a basis for the theory of the instincts in biology. On the ground of a far-reaching consideration of the processes which go to make up life and which lead to death, it becomes probable that we should recognize the existence of two classes of instincts, corresponding to the contrary processes of construction and dissolution in the organism. On this view, the one set of instincts, which work essentially in silence, would be those which follow the aim of leading the living creature to death and therefore deserve to be called the "*death instincts*"; these would be directed outwards as the result of the combination of numbers of unicellular elementary organisms, and would manifest themselves as *destructive* or *aggressive* impulses. The other set of instincts would be those which are better known to us in analysis—the libidinal, sexual or life instincts, which are best comprised under the name of *Eros*; their purpose would be to form living substance into ever greater unities, so that life may be prolonged and brought to higher development. . . . Life would consist in the manifestations of the conflict or interaction between the two classes of instincts.'[1] (See also below, History of the Development of Instinct Theory, and concept: The Death Instinct.)

Thus, after he put forward this theory,[2] Freud was considering instincts on two levels: the biological, whose source is to be found in the somatic organization, and the psychical. The psychical level could be further subdivided into the psychological drives, in themselves inaccessible to study, and ideational representatives of these drives, knowable through the ego. Describing the 'mental provinces' in structural terms, Freud said of the id:

[1] (1923a) 'Two Encyclopaedia Articles', S.E., Vol. 18, p. 258–9.
[2] (1920g) *Beyond the Pleasure Principle*, S.E., Vol. 18.

'It contains everything that is inherited, that is present at birth, that is laid down in the constitution—above all, therefore, the instincts, which originate from the somatic organization and which find a first psychical expression here [in the id] in forms unknown to us.'[1]

Of the way in which the ego performs its task of self-preservation, he says:

'As regards *internal* events, in relation to the id, it performs that task by gaining control over the demands of the instincts, by deciding whether they are to be allowed satisfaction, by postponing that satisfaction to times and circumstances favourable in the external world, or by suppressing their excitations entirely.'[2]

III. THE HISTORICAL DEVELOPMENT OF INSTINCT THEORY

Summary

The development of instinct theory may be divided into four main phases according to the groups of instinct distinguished by Freud at different times:

Phase One

1894–1911: In this phase Freud accepted the then current distinction made by biologists between the self-preservative instinct, tending towards the preservation of the individual, and the sexual instincts, tending towards the preservation of the species. However, this phase requires a further subdivision:

(a) *1894–97:* During these years Freud's assumption of opposing biological drives, self-preservative and sexual, was implicit, but not discussed. At this period, what he put forward was essentially an affect theory, and his discussion of mental conflict was in terms of opposing 'ideas' or 'wishes'. Though he already emphasized the importance of sexuality, his emphasis was still heavily on external traumata and physical events, in the form of seduction, as the origin of mental conflicts.

(b) *1897–1911:* With the discovery of the oedipus complex, and the

---

[1] (1940a [1938]) *An Outline of Psycho-Analysis*, S.E., Vol. 23, p. 145.
[2] ibid., pp. 145–6.

realization of the importance of phantasy life in mental conflict, the significance of external traumata and physical events was dimished. In this phase Freud found it necessary to move away from the physical to the psychical, and concentrated on the psychological aspects of instinctual drives, of which the 'ideas' and 'wishes' found in mental conflict were now seen to be derivatives. He postulated a conflict between the sexual, or libidinal instincts and self-preservative instincts, to which, in 1910, he gave the name 'ego-instincts'. At this phase of his theory this conflict was equated with one between the conscious and unconscious forces in the mind, the ego being thought of as conscious. The ego-instincts, subserving the self-preservative needs of the ego, were the repressing force, the sexual instincts the repressed force, striving towards conscious-ness and satisfaction.

Most of Freud's major postulates about the sexual instincts were laid down at this time, but little work was done on the ego instincts, which remained obscure.

Phase Two: 1911–14
The introduction to the concept of narcissism blurred the dis-tinction between the sexual and the ego instincts, since it now seemed that they had a common, libidinal origin. A distinction could be made only in terms of the object on to which the libido was directed, i.e. an external object or the own ego. However, Freud still thought that besides the libidinal component of the ego instincts, there was also a non-libidinal one, which he termed 'interest'.

Phase Three: 1915–20
In this phase aggression, previously considered to be a component of the sexual instinct, and considered mainly in the context of sadism, was now ascribed by Freud to the non-libidinal ego-instincts, in the form of the instinct for mastery over the external world. This greater emphasis on the importance of aggression arose out of Freud's consideration of ambivalence, the opposition between love and hate.

Phase Four: 1920–39
In this phase the antithesis between the sexual and the aggressive instincts was maintained, but they now became part of larger

entities, respectively the life and death instincts. The self-preservative instincts were grouped with the sexual instincts as part of the life instinct. Aggression was no longer considered as belonging to the ego-instincts.

Thus, the theory remained throughout a dualistic one, although there was one short period (Phase Two: 1911–14) when Freud thought his discoveries might necessitate the assumption of a monistic theory. What changed were the categories of instincts he assumed. (The dates given for these phases are somewhat arbitrary, since there was always a period of transition, when the beginnings of new ideas and formulations begin to appear in his writings. In general the date of a key paper is used to indicate a turning point in the theory.)

Phase One: 1894–1911
(a) *1894–7: Quality of Sexual and Self-Preservative Instincts Implicit*

The term 'instinct' is not to be found in Freud's published works during this period, though it occurs once in the posthumously published 'Project'[1] and once in Breuer's contribution to the *Studies on Hysteria.*[2] At this time Freud's attention was not directed to the study of instincts as such.* He implicitly assumed the existence of sexual and self-preservative drives, which he viewed as sources of constant somatic stimulation operating within the organism. The organism is governed by the tendency to keep excitation as low as possible so as to avoid unpleasurable tension. In the 'Project' this tendency is referred to as the 'principle of neuronic inertia', the tendency of the neuronic system to divest itself of 'quantity' and so to keep itself free from stimulation.[3] Freud translated the neurological idea of 'quantity' into the psychological one of 'quota of affect' or 'sum of excitation'.

'. . . in mental functions something is to be distinguished—a quota of affect or a sum of excitation—which possesses all the characteristics of a quantity (though we have no means of measuring it),

---

* He thought of mental conflict at this time in terms of affects which come into conflict with each other and which have to be defended against.

[1] (1950a [1887–92]) 'A Project for a Scientific Psychology', in *The Origins of Psycho-Analysis*, Imago, London, p. 379.

[2] (1895d) *Studies on Hysteria*, S.E., Vol. 2, p. 200.

[3] (1950a [1887– 92]) *The Origins of Psycho-Analysis*, Imago, London, p. 356 n.

which is capable of increase, diminution, displacement and discharge, and which is spread over the memory-traces of ideas somewhat as an electric charge is spread over the surface of a body'.[1]

Although he was already moving away from neurological to psychological lines of thought, Freud's theory of neurosis at this time still places great emphasis on physical events, either past or present. In the case of the 'actual' neuroses, it was a current abnormality of the sexual life giving rise to somatic tension through lack of discharge. In the psychoneuroses it was a traumatic event in childhood, a sexual seduction which had given rise to genital excitation.

'... each of the major neuroses which I have enumerated has as its immediate cause one particular disturbance of the economics of the nervous system, and ... these functional pathological modifications *have as their common source the subject's sexual life, whether they lie in a disorder of his contemporary sexual life or in important events in his past life.*'[2]
'... *a precocious experience of sexual relations with actual excitement of the genitals, resulting from sexual abuse committed by another person;* and *the period of life* at which this fatal event takes place is *earliest youth*—the years up to the age of eight or ten, before the child has reached sexual maturity'.[3]

Psychoneurotic conflict occurred, he said then, because of the arousal of 'incompatible' ideas or wishes, invariably of a sexual nature, which were unacceptable to the ego because of their accompanying distressing affect. These ideas come into association with unconscious memory traces of infantile sexual traumata, and produce excitatory processes in the genitals similar to those produced by the sexual experience itself. The ego defends against these ideas by repression and by separating them from their effect. Symptoms are the compromise resulting from the conflict between the ego and these ideas. At this time Freud thought that the processes involved in repression might be physical rather than unconscious psychical ones.

[1] (1894a) 'The Neuro-Psychoses of Defence', S.E., Vol. 3, p. 60.
[2] (1896a) 'Heredity and the Aetiology of the Neuroses', S.E., Vol. 3, p. 149.
[3] ibid., p. 152.

'It is known that having ideas with a sexual content produces excitatory processes in the genitals which are similar to those produced by sexual experience itself. We may assume that this somatic excitation becomes transposed to the psychical sphere.'[1]

'*The defence achieves its purpose of thrusting the incompatible idea out of consciousness if there are infantile sexual scenes present in the (hitherto normal) subject in the form of unconscious memories, and if the idea that is to be repressed can be brought into logical or associative connection with an infantile experience of that kind.*'[2]

'The separation of the sexual idea from its affect and the attachment of the latter to another, suitable but not incompatible idea— these are processes which occur without consciousness. Their existence can only be presumed, but cannot be proved by any clinico-psychological analysis. Perhaps it would be more correct to say that these processes are not of a psychical nature at all, that they are physical processes whose psychical consequences present themselves as if what is expressed by the terms "separation of an idea from its affect" and "false connection" of the latter had really taken place'.[3]

Later Freud clarified that these ideas or wishes were to be understood as derivatives of sexual instincts.

'Psychoanalytic research traces back the symptoms of patients' illnesses with really surprising regularity to impressions from their *erotic life*. It shows us that the pathogenic wishful impulses are in the nature of erotic instinctual components.'[4]

'Our attention has been drawn to the importance of the instincts in ideational life. We have discovered that every instinct tries to make itself effective by activating ideas that are in keeping with its aims.'[5]

[1] (1896b) 'Further Remarks on the Neuro-Psychoses of Defence', S.E., Vol. 3, p. 166 n.
[2] (1896c) 'The Aetiology of Hysteria', S.E., Vol. 3, p. 211.
[3] (1894a) 'The Neuro-Psychoses of Defence', S.E., Vol. 3, p. 53.
[4] (1910a) 'Five Lectures on Psycho-Analysis', S.E., Vol. 11, p. 40.
[5] (1910i) 'The Psycho-Analytic View of Psychogenic Disturbances of Vision', S.E., Vol. 11, p. 213.

(b) *1897–1911: Duality of Sexual and Ego instincts Made Explicit*
The realization that the childhood seductions reported by his patients were not reality events but fantasies, and Freud's discovery of the universality of the oedipus complex led to a drastic shift of emphasis.[1] External seductions leading to genital excitation were now regarded as less important. What was important was the fantasy life from which were derived the ideas and wishes, whose significance he had already emphasized.

'Since then I have learned to explain a number of phantasies of seduction as attempts at fending off memories of the subject's *own* sexual activity (infantile masturbation). When this point had been clarified, the "traumatic" element in the sexual experiences of childhood lost its importance and what was left was the realization that infantile sexual activity (whether spontaneous or provoked) prescribes the direction that will be taken by later sexual life after maturity. . . . After I had made this correction, "infantile sexual traumas" were in a sense replaced by "the infantilism of sexuality".'[2]

In discussing the sexual instincts, Freud had, of necessity, to take into account their somatic origin, and he also put forward a chemical theory of sexual excitation.[3] But in the main he concentrated on the psychical processes involved.

In this period he studied the sexual instincts closely, but there was little mention of the self-preservative, or ego-instincts, except insofar as he compares them with the sexual instincts, or mentions their influence on or interference with the sexual instincts, e.g.:

'The fact of the existence of sexual needs in human beings and animals is expressed in biology by the assumption of a "sexual instinct", on the analogy of the instinct of nutrition, that is of hunger. Everyday language possesses no counterpart to the word "hunger", but science makes use of the word "libido" for that purpose.'[4]

---

[1] (1950a [1885–1902]) *The Origins of Psycho-Analysis*, Imago, London, letters 69 (21.9.97) and 71 (15.10.97), pp. 215 and 223.

[2] (1906a) 'My Views on the Part Played by Sexuality in the Aetiology of the Neuroses', S.E., Vol. 8, p. 274 n.

[3] (1905d) *Three Essays on the Theory of Sexuality*, S.E., Vol. 7, p. 216 n.

[4] ibid., p. 135.

'Opposition between ideas is only an expression of struggles between the various instincts. From the point of view of our attempted explanation, a quite specially important part is played by the undeniable opposition between the instincts which subserve sexuality, the attainment of sexual pleasure, and those other instincts, which have as their aim the self-preservation of the individual—the ego-instincts.

'. . . The sexual and ego-instincts alike have in general the same organs and systems of organs at their disposal. Sexual pleasure is not attached merely to the function of the genitals. . . . The saying that it is not easy for anyone to serve two masters is thus confirmed. The closer the relation into which an organ with a dual function of this kind enters with *one* of the major instincts, the more it withholds itself from the other. This principle is bound to lead to pathological consequences if the two fundamental instincts are disunited and if the ego maintains a repression of the sexual component instinct concerned.'[1]

The last quoted reference is also the first time that Freud used the term 'ego-instincts' and equated them with the self-preservative instincts.

That Freud's attention was directed first of all to the sexual instincts was due to his early work being with hysteria and obsessional neurosis, whose basis he saw as a conflict over sexuality.

'In the course of investigating the neuroses we came to know the ego as the restricting and repressing power and the sexual trends as the restricted and repressed one; we therefore believed that we had clear evidence not only of the difference between the two groups of instincts but also of the conflict between them. The first object of our study was only the sexual instincts, whose energy we named "libido".'[2]

The first published use of the term 'libido' occurs in 1895.[3] Prior to that it is used in the Fliess correspondence.[4]

[1] (1910i) 'The Psycho-Analytic View of Psychogenic Disturbance of Vision', S.E., Vol. 11, pp. 213–16.

[2] (1933a) *New Introductory Lectures on Psycho-Analysis*, S.E., Vol. 22, p. 96.

[3] (1895b) 'On the Grounds for Detaching a Particular Syndrome from Neurasthenia under the Description "Anxiety Neurosis"', S.E., Vol. 3.

[4] (1950a [1887–1902]) *The Origins of Psycho-Analysis*, Imago, London, Drafts E and F, 1894, pp. 88 and 96.

The majority of Freud's formulations on the sexual instincts were put forward in detail in 1905 in the *Three Essays*.[1] (A number of these had been adumbrated in earlier papers or letters to Fliess.) But some important sections were added in subsequent editions, belonging to later phases in the development of instinct theory, to bring the book up to date. To this period, however, belong his discussion of the theories of infantile sexuality, bisexuality, the thesis of the component instincts and erotogenic zones, the auto-erotic and object-directed stages of the libido, and the genital organization of the libido. Later additions include the concept of the various pre-genital organizations of the libido, (1913, anal phase; 1915, oral phase; 1923, phallic phase) and the introduction of the stage of narcissism, in between the autoerotic and object-directed stages of libido (1911). The time at which libido was directed outwards on to an external object was then shifted back from puberty to infancy, whereas previously Freud had characterized sexuality as autoerotic and objectless until puberty. Though he discussed the vicissitudes of libido in 1905, the actual section on the libido theory[2] was not added until 1915, after the introduction of the concept of narcissism.

Infantile Sexuality: In an editorial note to the *Three Essays* Strachey comments that Freud was not immediately reconciled to his discovery of infantile sexuality.[3] Strachey points out some contradictory passages in *The Interpretation of Dreams*.

'Though we think highly of the happiness of childhood because it is still innocent of sexual desires, we should not forget what a fruitful source of disappointment and renunciation, and consequently what a stimulus to dreaming, may be provided by the other of the two great vital instincts.'[4]

'We learn from them [psychoneurotics] that a child's sexual wishes—if in their embryonic stage they deserve to be so described—awaken very early.'[5]

Apart from this, further confusion can be avoided if it is borne in mind that at first Freud thought of sexuality as remaining more

---

[1] (1905d) *Three Essays on the Theory of Sexuality*, S.E., Vol. 7.
[2] ibid. [1915], p. 217 n.   [3] ibid., Ed. note p. 127.
[4] (1900a) *The Interpretation of Dreams*, S.E., Vol. 4, p. 130.   [5] ibid., p. 257.

or less dormant until puberty, unless accidentally stimulated. Such activity as there was, was autoerotic. For example, in the first paper published after his discovery of the oedipus complex, and in which he still emphasizes the importance of seduction, he states:

'We do wrong to ignore the sexual life of children entirely; in my experience, children are capable of every psychical sexual activity, and many somatic sexual ones as well. Just as the whole human sexual apparatus is not comprised in the external genitals and the two reproductive glands, so human sexual life does not begin only with puberty, as on a rough inspection it may appear to do. Nevertheless it is true that the organization and evolution of the human species strives to avoid any great degree of sexual activity during childhood. It seems that in man the sexual instinctual forces are meant to be stored up so that, on their release at puberty, they may serve great cultural ends. Consideration of this sort may make it possible to understand why the sexual experiences of childhood are bound to have a pathogenic affect. But they produce their effect only to a very slight degree at the time at which they occur; what is far more important is their *deferred* effect, which can only take place at later periods of growth. This deferred effect originates— as it can do in no other way—in the psychical traces which have been left behind by infantile sexual experiences. During the interval between the experiences of those impressions and their reproduction (or rather, the reinforcement of the libidinal impulses which proceed from them), not only the somatic sexual apparatus but the psychical apparatus as well has undergone an important development; and thus it is that the influence of these earlier sexual experiences now leads to an abnormal psychical reaction, and psychopathological structures come into existence.'[1]

In 1905 Freud corrected this view that sexuality is normally latent until puberty and arousable only through external influence:

'. . . infantile amnesia, which turns everyone's childhood into something like a prehistoric epoch and conceals from him the beginnings of his sexual life, is responsible for the fact that in general no importance is attached to childhood in the development of sexual life'.[2]

---

[1] (1898a) 'Sexuality in the Aetiology of the Neuroses', S.E., Vol. 3, pp. 280–1.
[2] (1905d) *Three Essays on the Theory of Sexuality*, S.E., Vol. 7, p. 176.

'Obviously seduction is not required in order to arouse a child's sexual life; that can also come about spontaneously from internal causes . . . under the influence of seduction children can become polymorphously perverse, and can be led into all possible kinds of sexual irregularities. This shows that an aptitude for them is innately present in their disposition. There is consequently little resistance towards carrying them out, since the mental dams against sexual excesses—shame, disgust and morality—have either not yet been constructed at all or are only in course of construction, according to the age of the child.'[1]

'Our study of thumb-sucking or sensual sucking has already given us the three essential characteristics of an infantile sexual manifestation . . . it has as yet no sexual object, and is thus auto-erotic; and its sexual aim is dominated by an erotogenic zone. It is to be anticipated that these characteristics will be found to apply equally to most of the other activities of the infantile sexual instincts.'[2]

Bisexuality: Freud put forward the view, at this time, that human beings are innately bisexual and that the psychological distinction between male and female is established only in puberty[3] (see Concepts: Bisexuality; Masculine-Feminine; Active-Passive).

Component Instincts and Erotogenic Zones: Freud postulated that sexuality is not a single instinct, but is composed of a number of component instincts, such as exhibitionism and scopophilia, sadism and masochism, which at first seek gratification independently of one another, until they are unified in the genital phase. The oral, anal and phallic component instincts, introduced at later phases in the development of instinct theory, are intimately linked with erotogenic zones, areas of the body capable of giving rise to pleasurable excitation (see Concepts: Component Instincts, Erotogenic Zones.)[4]

The Autoerotic and Object-directed Stages of the Libido; The Genital Phase: In 1905, Freud described childhood sexuality as for the most part objectless and autoerotic, each component instinct seeking gratification separately on parts of the child's own body. Only

[1] ibid., pp. 190–1.   [2] ibid., pp. 182–3.   [3] ibid., p. 219 n.
[4] ibid., pp. 162, 167 f, 183–7, 207.

at puberty, he thought, were the component instincts united under the primacy of the genital zone, subserving reproduction and directed on to another person as sexual object. These early views are summarized in a 1915 addition to the *Three Essays* (see Concepts: Autoerotism, The Genital Phase, Libidinal Development at Puberty).[1] He noted, however, that certain of the component instincts, scopophilia and exhibitionism, from the first involve other people as objects. These, he thought, might originally arise from sources independent of sexuality (see Concepts: Scopophilia, Exhibitionism).[2]

With the introduction of the concept of narcissism in the next phase of his theory Freud revised his view of childhood sexuality as objectless and autoerotic, now recognizing that even in infancy first the self, then other persons are taken as objects (see Concept: Narcissism).

It was not until later that Freud described the pregenital phases of libidinal organization, in which the component instincts have come together, in childhood, and are directed on to an external object, but the dominant erotogenic zone is not the genital one. The oral phase is first described in a 1915 addition to the *Three Essays*[3] where is also mentioned the anal phase, though this was first mentioned two years earlier.[4] The phallic phase, where the dominant zone is the genital, but only the male genital is recognized, was added only in 1923 (see Concepts: Oral, Anal and Phallic Phases, Latency).[5] Fixations of libido can occur at any of these stages, thus paving the way for regression back to early stages of organization when later neutoric conflicts occur (see Concepts: Fixation, Regression).

PHASE TWO, 1911–14: INTRODUCTION OF THE CONCEPT NARCISSISM

Freud's study of homosexuality and paranoia led to the postulation of the stage of narcissism in libidinal development (see Concept: Narcissism). As early as 1910 there are references to the narcissistic basis of object-choice.[6] In his paper on the Schreber case he

---

[1] (1905d [1915]) *Three Essays on the Theory of Sexuality*, S.E., Vol. 7, p. 197.
[2] ibid., pp. 192–3.   [3] ibid. [1915], p. 198.
[4] (1931i) 'The Disposition to Obsessional Neurosis', S.E., Vol. 12, pp. 320–1.
[5] (1923e) 'The Infantile Genital Organization of the Libido', S.E., Vol. 19.
[6] (1905d [1910]) *Three Essays on the Theory of Sexuality*, S.E., Vol. 7, p. 144 n.

describes the stage of primary narcissism, the phenomenon of regression to this stage, in which object cathexes are withdrawn on to the ego, and discusses the problems this new postulate poses. The conclusions to be drawn from the discovery of narcissism were difficult to reconcile with the theory of the division between sexual and ego instincts.

'Recent investigations have directed our attention to a stage in the development of libido which it passes through on the way from auto-erotism to object-love. This stage has been given the name of narcissism. What happens is this. There comes a time in the development of the individual at which he unifies his sexual instincts (which have hitherto been engaged in auto-erotic activities) in order to obtain a love-object; and he begins by taking himself, his own body, as his love-object. . . . This half-way phase between autoerotism and object-love may perhaps be indispensable normally'.[1]

In this period Freud gave increasing attention to the ego-instincts, though he remained dissatisfied with the state of psycho-analytic knowledge of them. The implications of the introduction of the stage of narcissism were further discussed in his paper on this topic.[2] Here he put forward the idea of an original cathexis of the ego with libido, which is only later directed on to objects. Thus it becomes hard to distinguish between libidinal and ego-instincts, at any rate until after there is object cathexis. Freud drew a distinction between ego-libido and object-libido, thus providing a new dichotomy in terms of the direction rather than the source of the instinct. He speaks of narcissism as:

'. . . the libidinal complement to the egoism of the instinct of self-preservation, a measure of which may justifiably be attributed to every living creature'.[3]

'Thus we form the idea of there being an original libidinal cathexis of the ego, from which some is later given off to objects, but which fundamentally persists and is related to the object-cathexes much

---

[1] (1911c) 'Psycho-Analytic Notes on an Autobiographical Account of a Case of Paranoia (Dementia Paranoides)', S.E., Vol. 12, p. 60 n.

[2] (1914c) 'On Narcissism: An Introduction', S.E., Vol. 14. [3] ibid., pp. 73-4.

as the body of an amoeba is related to the pseudopodia which it puts out.'[1]

'We see also, broadly speaking, an antithesis between ego-libido and object-libido. The more the one is employed, the more the other becomes depleted. . . . Finally, as regards the differentiation of psychical energies, we are led to the conclusion that to begin with, during the state of narcissism, they exist together and that our analysis is too coarse to distinguish between them; not until there is object-cathexis is it possible to discriminate a sexual energy—the libido—from an energy of the ego-instincts. . . . if we grant the ego a primary cathexis of libido, why is there any necessity for further distinguishing a sexual libido from a non-sexual energy of the ego-instincts? Would not the postulation of a single kind of psychical energy save us all the difficulties of differentiating an energy of the ego-instincts from ego-libido, and ego-libido from object-libido?'[2]

'A differentiation of libido into a kind which is proper to the ego and one which is attached to objects is an unavoidable corollary to an original hypothesis which distinguished between sexual instincts and ego-instincts.'[3]

'I should like at this point expressly to admit that the hypothesis of separate ego-instincts and sexual instincts (that is to say, the libido theory) rests scarcely at all upon a psychological basis, but derives its principal support from biology. But I shall be consistent enough [with my general rule] to drop this hypothesis if psycho-analytic work should itself produce some other, more serviceable hypothesis about the instincts.'[4]

Thus we can see that in spite of the apparent blurring of the distinction between ego and sexual instincts, Freud's clinical experience, as well as current biological assumptions, made him feel it was necessary to maintain the distinction, though prepared to give it up should a better solution offer itself. The section on the libido theory added to the *Three Essays* in 1915 reflects the views

[1] (1914c) 'On Narcissism: An Introduction', S.E., Vol. 14. p. 75.
[2] ibid., p. 76.   [3] ibid., p. 77.   [4] ibid., p. 79.

stated above, and Freud there refers to the ego as the original reservoir of libido, from which later object cathexes are sent out.[1]

PHASE THREE, 1915–20: AGGRESSION AS AN EGO-INSTINCT

A further development in Freud's theory is to be found in his paper on 'Instincts and their Vicissitudes'.[2] He here reiterates the distinction between the ego instincts and sexual instincts, which is to be regarded only as a working hypothesis,[3] and notes again that the sexual instincts are originally attached to the instincts of self-preservation.[4]

In discussing instinctual vicissitudes he comes to the problem of the relationship between love and hate, which, he concludes, are not to be thought of as instincts, but as affects, or attitudes of the ego. (It should be borne in mind that in the papers of this period, prior to the introduction of the structural theory, Freud uses the term 'ego' most often to mean 'self'.)

'. . . the attitudes of love and hate cannot be made use of for the relations of *instincts* to their objects, but are reserved for the relations of the *total ego* to objects.'[5]

Freud distinguishes various antitheses concerning loving and hating. One, loving and hating together versus indifference is found at the very beginning of mental life, at the stage of primary narcissism, when only the self is cathected and the external world is indifferent for purposes of satisfaction.

But since the self cannot long avoid feeling internal instinctual stimuli as unpleasurable, and it soon has to acquire objects from the external world to satisfy its self-preservative instincts. The polarity loving versus hating arises still in the stage of primary narcissism, when the ego incorporates into itself pleasurable parts of the external world and projects the unpleasurable parts of itself on to the external world. Thus making the self coincide once more with what is pleasurable and the external world with unpleasure. The 'ego' loves itself and hates the external world with its unwelcome influx of stimuli.[6]

---

[1] (1905d [1915]) *Three Essays on the Theory of Sexuality*, S.E., Vol. 7, p. 217 f.
[2] (1915c) 'Instincts and Their Vicissitudes', S.E., Vol. 14.   [3] ibid., p. 124.
[4] ibid., p. 126.   [5] ibid., p. 137.   [6] ibid., p. 135 f.

When the stage of narcissism gives way to object love, the ego seeks to incorporate into itself objects which give pleasure, and seeks to repel unpleasurable objects in the same way as it originally took flight from unwelcome external stimuli.

'We feel the "repulsion" of the object, and hate it; this hate can afterwards be intensified to the point of an aggressive inclination against the object—an intention to destroy it.'[1]

Freud describes how, in the course of development 'love' comes to denote the pleasure relation of the ego to objects, and how it finally becomes fixed to sexual objects. Hate, however, is not intimately connected with sexual pleasure, but rather with the ego instincts.

'The relation of *unpleasure* seems to be the sole decisive one. The ego hates, abhors and pursues with intent to destroy all objects which are a source of unpleasurable feelings for it, without taking into account whether they mean a frustration of sexual satisfaction or of the satisfaction of self-preservative needs. Indeed, it may be asserted that the true prototypes of the relation of hate are derived not from sexual life, but from the ego's struggle to preserve and maintain itself. . . . Hate, as a relation to objects, is older than love. It derives from the narcissistic ego's primordial repudiation of the external world with its outpouring of stimuli. As an expression of the reaction of pleasure evoked by objects, it always remains in an intimate relation with the self-preservative instincts; so that sexual and ego-instincts can readily develop an antithesis which repeats that of love and hate.'[2]

Freud here propounded an aggressive propensity (though not yet a separate instinct), which is not a component of the sexual instinct, but which belongs to the self-preservative instinct. He also spoke of a 'general ego-interest', and so reaffirmed the existence of non-libidinal drives.

'We termed the cathexes of energy which the ego directs towards the objects of its sexual desires "libido"; all the others, which are sent out by the self-preservative instincts, we termed "interest".[3]

[1] (1915c) 'Instincts and Their Vicissitudes,' S.E. ,Vol. 14. p. 137.
[2] ibid., p. 138 f.
[3] (1916–17) *Introductory Lectures on Psycho-Analysis*, S.E., Vol. 6, p. 414.

'. . . How do we differentiate between the concepts of narcissism and egoism? Well, narcissism, I believe, is the libidinal complement to egoism. When we speak of egoism, we have in view only the individual's *advantage*; when we talk of narcissism we are also taking his libidinal satisfaction into account.'[1]

This position was maintained until the drastic revision which took place in the next phase of the theory.

Phase Four

(a) *1920–39: Duality of Life and Death Instincts* The final phase in Freud's theory of instincts was reached in 1920 when he drastically revised the theory.[2] Evidence from the traumatic neuroses, dreams and the transference situation in analysis showed the compulsion to repeat experiences from which there was no possibility of deriving pleasure, and which could never, in the past, have provided instinctual satisfaction. It was necessary, therefore, to conclude the existence of a repetition-compulsion which overrides the pleasure principle, hitherto considered to be the dominating tendency of the mental life.[3] (For a fuller discussion see Concept: The Death Instinct; see also Concepts: The Principles of Mental Functioning, Freud considered that the tendency to repeat was an instinctual characteristic:

'*It seems, then, that an instinct is an urge inherent in organic life to restore an earlier state of things* which the living entity has been obliged to abandon under the pressure of external disturbing forces; that is, it is a kind of organic elasticity, or, to put it another way, the expression of the inertia inherent in organic life.'[4]

He adduces biological evidence to support this view,[5] and puts forward the theory of opposing life and death instincts. Both instincts would be primitive biological ones and they would have arisen at the time of the emergence of organic from inorganic matter. In the death, or destructive instinct, then, the compulsion to repeat would take the form of the tendency to return to the inorganic state. In Eros, the life instinct, it would take the form of the tendency to pursue the development of life and to repeat the process of creation of life. The sexual instinct would thus be 'the

---

[1] ibid., p. 417.   [2] (1920g) *Beyond the Pleasure Principle*, S.E., Vol. 18.
[3] ibid., pp. 9–11, 19–23, 27–35.   [4] ibid., p. 36.   [5] ibid., pp. 36–8.

true life instinct' and the polarity life—death instinct would parallel the love-hate polarity.[1] Freud discussed this theory in terms of primitive organisms and individual cells. In a footnote he succinctly summarizes the previous development of instinct theory, and shows how these new postulates can help in solving the problem of the classification of instincts.

'. . . With the hypothesis of narcissistic libido and the extension of the concept of libido to the individual cells, the sexual instinct was transformed for us into Eros, which seeks to force together and hold together the portions of living substance. What are commonly called the sexual instincts are looked upon by us as the part of Eros which is directed towards objects. . . . It is not so easy, perhaps, to follow the transformations through which the concept of the 'ego instincts' has passed. To begin with we applied that name to all the instinctual trends (of which we had no closer knowledge) which could be distinguished from the sexual instincts directed towards an object; and we opposed the ego instincts to the sexual instincts of which the libido is the manifestation. Subsequently we came to closer grips with the analysis of the ego and recognized that a portion of the 'ego instincts' is also of a libidinal character and has taken the subject's own ego as its object. These narcissistic self-preservative instincts had thenceforward to be counted among the libidinal sexual instincts. The opposition between the ego instincts and the sexual instincts was transformed into one between the ego instincts and the object instincts, both of a libidinal nature. But in its place a fresh opposition appeared between the libidinal (ego and object) instincts and others, which must be presumed to be present in the ego and which may perhaps actually be observed in the destructive instincts. Our speculations have transformed this opposition into one between the life instincts (Eros) and the death instincts.'[2]

This new formulation of instinct theory also made possible a better understanding of sadism and masochism. This aspect was mentioned in *Beyond the Pleasure Principle*, but taken up more fully in later papers. Sadism had previously been thought of as an aggressive component of the libido, and masochism as a secondary

[1] (1920g) *Beyond the Pleasure Principle*, S.E., Vol. 18. pp. 38–40.
[2] ibid., p. 60 n.

phenomenon, resulting from a turning round on the self of sadism (see Concepts: Sadism, Masochism).[1]

'But how can the sadistic instinct, whose aim it is to injure the object, be derived from Eros, the preserver of life? Is it not plausible to suppose that this sadism is in fact a death instinct which, under the influence of the narcissistic libido, has been forced away from the ego and has consequently only emerged in relation to the object?'[2]

Now masochism was considered to be a primary phenomenon, evidence of the working of the death instinct within the individual. Part of the instinct remains within the organism but in order to preserve the life of the individual, it has to be bound by the libido, the life instinct, thus producing an 'original, erotogenic masochism'. Part is diverted outward in the service of the sexual function —sadism proper (see Concepts: Sadism, Masochism, Aggression).[3]

The Concept of Fusion: Freud stated that the concept of fusion was an indispensable assumption in instinct theory. Clearly, the individual would quickly die if the death instinct were not bound or neutralized by the life instinct. Though he occasionally used such phrases as 'a pure culture of the death instinct'.[4] This is evidently a looseness of phraseology, referring to the fact that in melancholia the death instinct may win the instinctual struggle. He made it quite clear that instincts are only to be found in fusions of varying proportions, e.g.:

'. . . The emergence of life would thus be the cause of the continuance of life and also at the same time of the strivings towards death; and life itself would be a conflict and compromise between these two trends. . . . This hypothesis throws no light whatever upon the manner in which the two classes of instincts are fused, blended, and alloyed with each other; but that this takes place regularly and very extensively is an assumption indispensable to our conception.'[5]

[1] (1915c) 'Instincts and their Vicissitudes', S.E., Vol. 14, p. 128 n.
[2] (1920g) *Beyond the Pleasure Principle*, S.E., Vol. 18, p. 54.
[3] (1924c) 'The Economic Problem of Masochism', S.E., Vol. 19, p. 163 n.
[4] (1923b) *The Ego and the Id*, S.E., Vol. 19, p. 53.   [5] ibid., pp. 40–1.

IV. THE INSTINCTS WITHIN THE MENTAL APPARATUS

Freud devoted much thought to the question of the function of the instincts within the mental apparatus, and the way in which this apparatus deals with them. His first psychological model of the mind, similar in many respects to the neurological one expounded in the 'Project', was put forward in Chapter Seven of *The Interpretation of Dreams*.[1] Here, he did not explicitly discuss the role of instincts within the mental apparatus, but dealt rather with the ideas and fantasies which arise as part of instinctual life.

But explicit references to the role of instincts within the mental apparatus were made in 1905[2] and are thereafter to be found throughout all phases of the development of the theory of instincts. The major formulations occur in the topographical structural models of the mind.

(a) *1905*

In *The Three Essays on the Theory of Sexuality* Freud was already giving thought to the mental forces which oppose instinctual expressions, e.g. he says:

'. . . the sexual instinct has to struggle against certain mental forces which act as resistances, and of which shame and disgust are the most prominent. It is permissible to suppose that these forces play a part in restraining that instinct within the limits that are regarded as normal; and if they develop in the individual before the sexual instinct has reached its full strength, it is no doubt that they will determine the course of its development.'[3]

'It is during this period of total or only partial latency that are built up the mental forces which are later to impede the course of the sexual instinct and, like dams, restrict its flow—disgust, feelings of shame and the claim of aesthetic and moral ideals.'[4]

(b) *The Topographical Theory*

A much fuller discussion of the role of instincts within the mental

---

[1] (1900a) *The Interpretation of Dreams*, S.E., Vol. 5.
[2] (1905d) *Three Essays on the Theory of Sexuality*, S.E., Vol. 7, pp. 162, 177.
[3] ibid., p. 162. [4] ibid., p. 177.

apparatus occurs in the metapsychological papers of 1915, where Freud puts forward his topographical theory.

In this model the mental apparatus is divided topographically into three systems, unconscious, preconscious and conscious.

'The nucleus of the *Ucs* consists of instinctual representatives which seek to discharge their cathexis; that is to say, it consists of wishful impulses. These instinctual impulses are co-ordinate with one another, exist side by side without being influenced by one another and are exempt from mutual contradiction. When two wishful impulses whose aims must appear to us incompatible become simultaneously active, the two impulses do not diminish each other or cancel each other out, but combine to form an intermediate aim, a compromise.'[1]

Ideas can be cathected by any of the three systems, but the instincts themselves cannot become objects of consciousness; only the ideational representatives of instincts can do this. On the other hand, emotions, feelings and affects cannot be unconscious, only the ideas to which they are attached can be repressed.[2]

Freud distinguishes between primal repression, by which the ideational representatives of instincts are denied access to consciousness, and repression proper, by which mental derivatives of, or trains of thought which have come into association with the repressed representatives are pushed out of consciousness. Repression does not effect the continued existence of the instinctual representative in the *Ucs* it interferes only with its relation to the *Cs*.[3]

For repression of instinctual representatives to occur, the motive force of unpleasure must be stronger than the pleasure obtained from satisfaction of an instinct. It cannot occur before there is a sharp cleavage between conscious and unconscious mental activity. Prior to this stage instincts are fended off by means of vicissitudes other than repression, such as reversal into the opposite, or turning round on the subject's own self.[4]

An instinctual representative develops with less interference and moves profusely if withdrawn from conscious influence. Derivatives which are sufficiently removed or distorted still have free

---

[1] (1915e) 'The Unconscious', S.E., Vol. 14, p. 186.   [2] ibid., p. 177 f.
[3] (1915d) 'Repression', S.E., Vol. 14, pp. 148–9.   [4] ibid., p. 147.

THE THEORY OF INSTINCTS

access to the *Cs*.[1] The production of symptoms and substitute formations indicate a return of the repressed. It is not repression itself that produces symptoms.[2] Different mechanism of substitute formation are found in the various neuroses.[3]

(c) The Structural Theory

In *The Ego and the Id*[4] Freud put forward the third model of the mind, in which the division into structures, id, ego and superego, partially replaces and supplements the older topographical division into conscious, preconscious and unconscious (see Concept: The Models of the Mind). The id becomes the seat of the instincts and is in conflict with the ego. But Freud emphasized that the ego can no longer be equated with the conscious, that is, the old conception of the conflict between instincts and ego as equivalent to a conflict between unconscious and consciousness no longer holds good.

'We have come upon something in the ego itself which is also unconscious, which behaves exactly like the repressed—that is, which produces powerful effects without itself being conscious and which requires special work before it can be made conscious. From the point of view of analytic practice, the consequence of this discovery is that we land in endless obscurities and difficulties if we keep to our habitual forms of expression and try, for instance, to derive neuroses from a conflict between the conscious and the unconscious. We shall have to substitute for this antithesis another, taken from our insight into the structural conditions of the mind—the antithesis between the coherent ego and the repressed which is split off from it.'[5]

'It is easy to see that the ego is that part of the id which has been modified by the direct influence of the external world through the medium of the *Pcpt-Cs*; in a sense it is an extension of the surface-differentiation. Moreover, the ego seeks to bring the influences of the external world to bear upon the id and its tendencies, and endeavours to substitute the reality principle for the pleasure principle which reigns unrestrictedly in the id. For the ego, perception plays the part which in the id falls to instinct. The ego

---

[1] (1915d) 'Repression', S.E., Vol. 14, p. 149..   [2] ibid., p. 154.
[3] ibid., pp. 154–6.   [4] (1923b) *The Ego and the Id*, S.E., Vol. 19.
[5] ibid., p. 17.

represents what may be called reason and common sense, in contrast to the id, which contains the passions.'[1]

As it develops, the ego gradually achieves the capacity to control and inhibit the instincts.[2] But the ego has to defend itself not only against the instincts of the id, but against dangers from two other directions—the external world and its own super-ego. The super-ego has arisen from an identification with the father at the time of the resolution of the oedipus complex, a process which involves desexualization of libido.[3]

Within the id, the death instincts work silently towards a reduction of tension, ultimately towards death. It is Eros which introduces tensions into the id, in the form of instinctual needs. Under the sway of the pleasure principle the id fends off these needs by striving for their satisfaction, especially for the discharge of sexual substances, the 'saturated vehicles' of erotic tensions, so that tension may be reduced.[4] Also within the id it is through the agency of Eros that the death instincts are libidinally bound and diverted on to the external world, thus preserving life.[5]

The ego assists the id in its efforts to reduce tension by sublimating some of the libido.[6] But processes of sublimation and desexualization also involve defusion—the death instincts are set free and the ego is then in danger from them. The process of super-ego formation involves such a defusion, and the destructiveness which is thus no longer bound becomes the source of the harshness of the ego-ideal. Thus id-contents reach the ego not only directly, but also by way of the ego-ideal.[7]

'The ego develops from perceiving instincts to controlling them, from obeying instincts to inhibiting them. In this achievement a large share is taken by the ego ideal, which indeed is partly a reaction-formation against the instinctual processes of the id. . . . Towards the two classes of instinct the ego's attitude is not impartial. Through its work of identification and sublimation it gives the death instincts in the id assistance in gaining control over the libido, but in so doing it runs the risk of becoming the objects of the death instincts and of itself perishing. In order to be able to help in this way it has had itself to become filled with libido; it thus

---

[1] ibid., p. 25.   [2] ibid., p. 56.   [3] ibid., pp. 54–6.   [4] ibid., p. 47.
[5] ibid., p. 41 and 46 m.   [6] ibid., p. 47.   [7] ibid., pp. 54–5.

itself becomes the representative of Eros and thenceforward desires to live and be loved.

'But since the ego's work of sublimation results in a defusion of the instincts and a liberation of the aggressive instincts in the super-ego, its struggle against the libido exposes it to the danger of mal-treatment and death. In suffering under the attacks of the super-ego or perhaps even succumbing to them, the ego is meeting with a fate like that of the protista which are destroyed by the products of decomposition that they themselves have created. From the econo-mic point of view the morality that functions in the super-ego seems to be a similar product of decomposition.'[1]

In putting forward these views Freud amended the theory of narcissism. Whereas he had previously considered the ego to be the 'reservoir' or narcissistic libido, he now stated that the id was this original reservoir, and the narcissism of the ego was only secondary.

'By thus getting hold of the libido from the object-cathexes, setting itself up as sole love-object, and de-sexualizing or sublimating the libido of the id, the ego is working in opposition to the purposes of Eros and placing itself at the service of the opposing instinctual impulses. . . . This would seem to imply an important amplifica-tion of the theory of narcissism. At the very beginning, all the libido of the id, the ego is working in opposition to the purposes of formation or is still feeble. The id sends part of this libido out into erotic object-cathexes, whereupon the ego, now grown stronger, tries to get hold of this object-libido and to force itself on the id as a love-object. The narcissism of the ego is thus a secondary one, which has been withdrawn from objects.'[2] (See, however, Concept: Narcissism, and Editor's Appendix to *The Ego and the Id*,[3] for a discussion of apparent contradictions in Freud's views on this subject.)

Freud returned to the subject of the apparent transformation of love into hate, which if it really occurred, would speak against the separation of the life and death instinct. But, he said, what really

---

[1] (1923b) *The Ego and the Id*, S.E., Vol. 19, pp. 55–7.   [2] ibid., p. 46.
[3] ibid., pp. 63–6.

occurs is a reactive displacement of neutralized cathexis. The store of desexualized libido is available for adding to either destructive or erotic instinctual impulses, and the case of the transformation of love into hate, this neutral energy is withdrawn from the erotic impulse and added to the hostile one.[1]

This new view of instincts made possible further insight into the role of the super-ego in obsessional neurosis and melancholia. If fusion of the two instincts occurs progressively with libidinal development, then the essence of regression lies in a defusion of instincts.[2] In the regression to the anal-sadistic phase which occurs in obsessional neurosis, destructive impulses towards the object are set free. Though the ego struggles against these impulses, the super-ego, whose own harshness derives from the destructive instincts, behaves as if the ego were responsible for the impulses, and 'reproaches' it. In melancholia, where the external object is not retained, the destructive instincts are all turned against the town ego.[3] (See also Concepts: Fusion-Defusion; Aggression.)

[1] ibid., pp. 42–5.   [2] ibid., p. 42.   [3] ibid., pp. 54–5.

COMPONENT INSTINCTS

Definition
Component instincts is the term used to designate any one of several different elements which by coming together and organizing themselves in special ways give shape to the final structure of the fully developed instinct. At the time these formulations were made Freud was referring specifically to the sexual instinct.

History
The theory of component instincts was first adumbrated in a letter to Fliess of December 6, 1896.[1] The term as such first appeared in the *Three Essays on the Theory of Sexuality*.[2] What is covered here refers mainly to the 'component instincts' of the 'sexual drive'.

The theory of 'component instincts' was derived from Freud's observation that the perversions are only made intelligible if the convergence of several motive forces was assumed: 'If such perversions admit of analysis, that is, if they can be taken to pieces, then they must be of a composite nature. This gives us a hint that perhaps the sexual instinct itself may be no simple thing, but put together from "components" which have come apart again in the perversions.'[3] 'A child's sexual life is indeed made up entirely of the activities of a number of component instincts which seek, independently of one another, to obtain pleasure, in part from the subject's own body and in part already from an external object.'[4]

In mature sexuality, some of the component instincts come to form part of what Freud named 'fore-pleasure', that is, when after having been predominantly auto-erotic and pursuing—independently of one another—certain types of pleasure as their sole sexual aim, they become subordinated under the primacy of the genital zone. The danger implicit here is that these 'fore-pleasure' activities, due to the excitation of the erotogenic zones, can take

[1] (1950a [1885–1902]) *The Origins of Psycho-Analysis*, Imago, London, 1954, pp. 73–81.
[2] (1905d) *Three Essays on the Theory of Sexuality*, S.E., Vol. 7, p. 166.
[3] ibid., p. 162.
[4] (1916–17) *Introductory Lectures on Psycho-Analysis*, S.E., Vol.15–16, p. 316.

the place of the normal sexual aim or 'end-pleasure', that is, the pleasure derived from the sexual act.[1]

Their source

'What we have called the component instincts of sexuality are either derived directly from these internal sources [Freud here implies a great number of internal processes out of which sexual excitation arises as a concomitant effect, as soon as the intensity of these processes passes beyond certain quantitative limits] or are composed of elements both from those sources and from the erotogenic zones.'[2]

'What distinguishes the instincts from one another and endows them with specific qualities is their relation to their somatic sources and to their aims. . . . There is a further provisional assumption. . . . It is to the effect that excitations of two kinds arise from the somatic organs. . . . One of these kinds of excitations we describe as being specifically sexual, and we speak of the organ concerned as the "erotogenic zone" of the sexual component instinct arising from it.'[3]

Order of emergence

In relation to the order of emergence of the component instincts Freud stated: 'The order in which the various instinctual impulses come into activity seems to be philo-genetically determined; so too does the length of time during which they are able to manifest themselves before they succumb to the effects of some freshly emerging instinctual impulse or to some typical repression [meaning here defence]. Variations, however, seem to occur both in temporal sequence and in duration, and these variations must exercise a determining influence upon the final result.'[4]

Their objects

Freud expressed the view that 'infantile sexual life, in spite of the preponderating dominance of erotogenic zones, exhibits components which from the very first involve other people as sexual objects. Such are the instincts of scopohilia, exhibitionism and cruelty, which appear in a sense independently of erotogenic zones; these instincts do not enter into intimate relations with genital life

---

[1] (1905d) *Three Essays on the Theory of Sexuality*, S.E., Vol. 7, p. 210 n.
[2] ibid., p. 205.   [3] ibid., p. 168.   [4] ibid., p. 241.

until later, but are already to be observed in childhood as independent impulses, distinct in the first instance from erotogenic sexual
activity'.[1] At a later stage Freud modified the formulation given
above, partly no doubt on account of the theory of *narcissism*,
which he had developed in the meantime. He says: 'For the
beginning of its activity the scopophilic instinct is auto-erotic: it
has indeed an object, but that object is part of the subject's own
body. It is only later that the instinct is led, by a process of comparison, to exchange this object for an analogous part of someone
else's body.'[2]

Freud remarks how the activity of the component instincts are
to start with auto-erotic, 'their object is negligible in comparison
with the organ which is their source, and as a rule coincides with
that organ. The object of the scopophilic instinct, however, though
it too is in the first instance a part of the subject's own body, is not
the eye itself; and in sadism the organic source, which is probably
the muscular apparatus . . . points unequivocally at an object
other than itself, even though that object is part of the subject's
own body'.[3] Freud further referred to the fact that the component
instincts frequently appear as a pair of opposites, one representing
the active and the other the passive part of the pair.[4]

Line of development from auto-erotism to object-love
An important line of development to be followed by the component instincts goes from auto-erotism to object love through
primary narcissism.

'There comes a time in the development of the individual at
which he unifies his sexual instincts (which have hitherto been
engaged in auto-erotic activities) in order to obtain a love-object;
and he begins by taking himself, his own body, as his love object
[here Freud is referring to primary narcissism], and only subsequently proceeds from this to the choice of some person other than
himself as his object.'[5]

One important source of confusion is due to not taking into
account the fact that Freud made it quite clear 'that the attitudes

[1] (1905d) *Three Essays on the Theory of Sexuality*, S.E. Vol. 7, p. 191 n.
[2] (1915c) 'Instincts and their Vicissitudes', S.E., Vol. 14, p. 130.
[3] ibid., p. 132.
[4] (1910a) 'Five Lectures on Psycho-Analysis', S.E., Vol. 11, p. 14.
[5] (1911c) 'Psycho-Analytic Notes on an Autobiographical Account of a Case
of Paranoia (Dementia Paranoides)', S.E., Vol. 12, p. 60.

of love and hate cannot be made use of for the relations of *instincts* to their objects, but are reserved for the relations of the *total ego* to objects'.[1]

Component instincts and libidinal phases of development

The different component instincts can be observed in connection with the libidinal phases of development. Freud says: 'We must regard each individual as possessing an oral erotism, an anal erotism, a urethral erotism, etc., and . . . the existence of mental complexes corresponding to these implies no judgment of abnormality or neurosis. The differences separating the normal from the abnormal can lie only in the relative strength of the individual components of the sexual instinct and in the use to which they are put in the course of development.'[2]

Constitution and component instincts

According to Freud one can distinguish a number of constitutions according to the innate preponderance of one or the other of the component instincts.[3]

'The hereditary sexual constitution presents us with a great variety of dispositions, according as one component instinct or another, alone or in combination with others, is inherited in particular strength.'[4]

Clinical applications

Normality and neuroses are closely linked with the developmental vicissitudes of the component instincts. '. . . The constitutional sexual disposition of children is incomparably more variegated than might have been expected . . . it deserves to be described as "polymorphously perverse" and . . . what is spoken of as the normal behaviour of the sexual function emerges from this disposition after certain of its components have been repressed . . . *normality* is a result of the repression of certain component instincts and constituents of the infantile disposition and of the subordination of the remaining constituents under the primacy of the genital zones . . . *perversions* correspond to disturbances of

---

[1] (1915c) 'Instincts and their Vicissitudes', S.E., Vol. 14, p. 137.
[2] (1905d) *Three Essays on the Theory of Sexuality.* S.E., Vol. 7, p. 205 n.
[3] ibid., p. 171.
[4] (1916–17) *Introductory Lectures on Psycho-Analysis*, S.E., Vol. 15–16, p. 362.

this coalescence owing to the overpowering and compulsive development of certain of the component instincts . . . *neuroses* can be traced back to an excessive repression of the libidinal trends.'[1]

And:

'An especially prominent part is played as factors in the formation of symptoms in psychoneuroses by the component instincts, which emerge for the most part as pairs of opposites. . . .'[2]

Vicissitudes

Freud described the possible vicissitudes of the component instincts. An instinct could be reversed into its opposite, that is, either a change from an active to a passive aim, for example, or on other occasions a reversal of its content (reaction formation); furthermore it could be turned round upon the self, repressed, sublimated, etc.[3] He further pointed out how certain traits of character, e.g. orderliness, parsimony and obstinacy, proceed from the dissipation of anal erotism and its employment in other ways, and how a similar connection exists between ambition and urethral erotism. Similarly other traits of character he thought would turn out to be either precipitates or reaction formations related to pregenital libidinal formations.[4] 'In the same way, the pathogenic significance of the constitutional factors must be weighed according to how much *more* of one component instinct than of another is present in the inherited disposition.'[5]

[1] (1906a) 'My Views on the Part Played by Sexuality in the Aetiology of the Neuroses', S.E., Vol. 7, p. 277.
[2] (1905d) *Three Essays on the Theory of Sexuality*, S.E., Vol. 7, p. 166.
[3] (1915c) 'Instincts and their Vicissitudes', S.E., Vol. 14, p. 126.
[4] (1933a) *New Introductory Lectures on Psycho-Analysis*, S.E., Vol. 22, p. 102 n.
[5] (1916–17) *Introductory Lectures on Psycho-Analysis*, S.E., Vol. 16, p. 374 n.

EROTOGENIC ZONES

1. *Definition*
An erotogenic zone 'is a part of the skin or mucous membrane in which stimuli of a certain sort evoke a feeling of pleasure possessing a particular quality. There can be no doubt that the stimuli which produce the pleasure are governed by special conditions, though we do not know what those are. A rhythmic character must play a part among them and the analogy of tickling is forced upon our notice. . . . There are predestined erotogenic zones, as is shown by the example of sucking. The same example, however, also shows us that any other part of the skin or mucous membrane can take over the functions of an erotogenic zone, and must therefore have some aptitude in that direction. Thus the quality of the stimulus has more to do with producing the pleasurable feeling than has the nature of the part of the body concerned. . . . Erotogenic and hysterogenic zones show the same characteristics.' [In a footnote added in 1915 he said: 'After further reflection and taking other observations into account, I have been led to ascribe the quality of erotogenicity to all parts of the body and to all the internal organs'].[1] 'We call the parts of the body that are important in the acquisition of sexual pleasure "erotogenic zones".'[2]

2. *History*
The first published use of the term *erotogenic zone* appears in the *Three Essays on Sexuality*, 1905. The conceptualization, however, was rather thoroughly developed in the years between 1896 and 1905[3] e.g. *Origins of P.A.*, letters 52, 55, and 75. *Jones* comments that the term *erotogenic zone* was 'undoubtedly coined on the model of the *hysterogenic zones*,' Freud noted that both types of zones shared the same characteristics.[4] The significance of erotogenic

---

[1] (1905d) *Three Essays on the Theory of Sexuality*, S.E., Vol. 7, p. 193 f.
[2] (1950a [1887–1902]) *The Origin of Psycho-Analysis*, Imago, London, 1954, p. 175 f., see also pp. 187 f., 232 f.
[3] (1910a) 'Five Lectures on Psycho-Analysis', S.E., Vol. 11, p. 44.
[4] Jones, E., *Sigmund Freud, Life and Works*, Hogarth Press, Vol. 2, p. 289 n.a. See also (1905d) *Three Essays on the Theory of Sexuality*, S.E., Vol. 7, p. 183 f.

zones seems to have been elucidated from growing clinical experience with perversions, hysterics and the evidence of the universal, active sexuality of childhood.[1] It is a basic concept since it provides one of the links between biology and the libido and instinct theories of psychoanalytic psychology.

3. Predestined erotogenic zones

Certain zones or areas of the body are in effect predestined by their anatomical juxtaposition to vital organs as to receive stimuli. These erotogenic zones are the oral, anal, urethral, clitoral and genital zones. These predestined zones of erotization are linked to 'great organic needs' such that the satisfaction of the related biological drives produces the concomitant effect of stimulating the erotogenic zone.[2]

4. Distinguishing characteristics of different zones

Freud remarked that the clearest distinction between one zone and another concerns the nature of the contrivance required for the satisfaction of the instinct.

(a) *Oral zone.* In the case of the labial zone it consisted of sucking [what is here referred to as the labial zone was later subsumed under the oral phase of libidinal development and was further subdivided into (1) the sucking stage and (2) the biting stage. Freud is here referring to the first stage of later division] and this will be replaced by other contrivances and muscular actions depending on the nature and position of the other erotogenic zones.[3] The labial (oral) zone is attached to the need for nourishment. Once the experience of pleasure has been established, as in sucking, it provides an impulse-need for the repetition of the experience. This is manifest in a peculiar feeling of tension, of itching or stimulation which is centrally conditioned and projected on to the peripheral erotogenic zone.[4] The early establishment of oral eroticism provides the avenue for the infant to explore its body as in example via the inclusion of the thumb for pleasure sucking which establishes a second, though inferior erotogenic zone.[5] (See Narcissism.)

(b) *The anal zone.* The anal zone is attached to processes of

---

[1] (1905d) *Three Essays on the Theory of Sexuality*, S.E., Vol. 7, p. 289.

[2] (1916–17) *Introductory Lectures on Psycho-Analysis*, S.E., Vol. 16, p. 315 f.

[3] (1905d) *Three Essays on the Theory of Sexuality*, S.E., Vol. 7, p. 185.

[4] ibid., p. 184.   [5] ibid., p. 182.

elimination and excretion. In relation to the anal zone Freud said:
'It is to be presumed that the erotogenic significance of this part of
the body is very great from the first'.[1]
(c) *The phallic zone.* The close connection of the glans and clitoris
with micturition is evident. According to Freud they do not play
the opening part and 'cannot be the vehicle of the oldest sexual
impulses but are destined to great things in the future' . . . being the
beginning of later normal sexual life.[2]

5. *The body as an erotogenic zone*
Other than the 'predestined zones', it was evident from the study of
hysteria that 'any other part of the skin or mucous membrane can
take over the functions of an erotogenic zone and must therefore
have some aptitude in that direction'.[3] By 1914, Freud had concluded that one could regard 'erotogenicity as a general characteristic
of all organs and [we] may then speak of an increase or decrease of it
in a particular part of the body'.[4]

6. *The relationship between erotogenic zones and component instincts*
There is a close connection between the concept erotogenic zones
and that of the component instincts. Freud assumed that in most
cases a given component instinct did arise from a specific erotogenic
zone. He suggested '. . . that excitation of two kinds arise from the
somatic organs, based upon differences of a chemical nature. One
of these kinds of excitation we describe as specifically sexual, and
we speak of the organ concerned as the "erotogenic zone" of the
sexual component instinct arising from it.' One ought to be
reminded here that Freud explicitly referred to the tentative nature
of these formulations but as he pointed out: . . . 'if I omitted all
mention of them, it would be impossible to say anything of substance about the instincts'.[5] In the *New Introductory Lectures* he
referred to the theory of instincts as our 'mythology'[6] and described
this type of discussion as 'biological psychology', that is the study
of the psychological concomitants of biological processes.[7] Finally
it is appropriate to note that according to Freud each 'component

[1] ibid., p. 185.   [2] ibid., p. 187.   [3] ibid., p. 183.
[4] (1914c) 'On Narcissism', S.E., Vol. 14, p. 84.   [5] (1905d [1915]) p. 168.
[6] (1933a) *New Introductory Lectures on Psycho-Analysis*, S.E., Vol. 22, p.
95 f.
[7] ibid., p. 96.

instinct is unalterably characterized by its *source*, that is, by the region or zone of the body from which its excitation is derived'.[1]

Gratification of the erotogenic impulse/itching occurs in early infancy without regard to psychological objects and with no other 'aim' than extinction of the excitation.[2] With the maturation of the infant's psychical life, the impulses of the erotogenic zones, which had been capable of independent satisfaction, became organized with respect to an object in the external world which is needed to gratify the impulse.[3] (See Source, Pressure, Aim and Object of the Sexual Component Instincts.)

7. Sources of excitation in the erotogenic zones

Excitation can be aroused by external sources, not least of which is the loving care of the mother which arouse excitation and provides gratification.[4] The erotogenic excitation may come either via internal stimuli incidental to general biological processes, or it may derive from external stimulation. But in both instances, the relief from excitation is to be found in yet another external stimulus or excitation which anomalously affords pleasure and gratification.[5] In time, the infant's affects and ideational processes will provide a third source of excitation. In all of these instances, gratification will be attended by manipulation/stimulation of erotogenic areas, by either child or external persons. Gratification is initially attained in each zone, such that oral, anal or urethral gratifications are not dependent on one another. Pubertal changes, however, mark a profound change both in the nature of the pleasure experienced[6] but also in the subordination of each zone to the dominant genital experience.[7] (See Libidinal Development at Puberty, Vol 1, p. 97.)

8. Function of erotogenic zones after adolescence

'The formula for the new function of the erotogenic zones runs therefore: they are used to make possible, through the medium of the fore-pleasure which can be derived from them (as it was during infantile life), the production of the greater pleasure of satisfac-

---

[1] (1923a) 'Two Encyclopaedia Articles', S.E., Vol. 18, p. 256.
[2] (1925j) 'Some Psychological Consequences of the Anatomical Distinction Between the Sexes', S.E., Vol. 19, p. 251.
[3] (1923a) 'Two Encyclopaedia Articles', S.E., Vol. 18, p. 256.
[4] (1905d) *Three Essays on the Theory of Sexuality*, S.E., Vol. 7, p. 223.
[5] ibid., p. 184.   [6] ibid., p. 210 f.   [7] ibid., p. 207. See also p. 235.

tion.'[1] The danger implicit is that these fore-pleasure activities can take the place of the sexual aim and the pleasure of satisfaction and that is in fact what happens in many perversions.[2]

9. *Erotogenic zones and constitution*

According to Freud 'it was possible to derive a multiplicity of innate sexual constitutions from variety in the development of the erotogenic zones . . . and that further help towards the differentiation of sexual constitutions may be found in the varying development of the individual sources of sexual excitation'.[3] Consequently everybody possesses oral, anal and urethral erotism, etc. The difference between normality and abnormality here can only lie in the relative strength of the individual components of the sexual instinct and in the use to which they are put in the course of development. In other words Freud took the view that there was another complementary series made out of the interaction between the innate sexual constitution and the environmental forces acting upon them.[4]

10. *Vicissitudes and clinical applications*

The erotogenic zones can suffer any one of several vicissitudes. The eroticism of the zones may become inactive with the transfer of libidinal cathexis to another zone,[5] because of maturational processes; because of repression and the reactive character traits that follow,[6] or because sublimation permits partial gratification via displacement.[7] The dominance of pregenital, erotogenic zonal excitation is characteristic of the perversions. Clinical work with hysterics most clearly demonstrated the remarkable plasticity of different zones and organs of the body to 'become the seat of new sensations and of changes in innervation'.[8] Freud has also referred to the pathogenic consequences of the erotization of both ego functions and the functions of body organs.[9] 'Not only is a large part of the symptomatology of hysteria derived directly from

---

[1] (1905d) *Three Essays on the Theory of Sexuality*, S.E., Vol. 7, p. 169.
[2] ibid., p. 211.   [3] ibid., p. 211.   [4] ibid., p. 205.
[5] [1920] ibid., p. 205 n.
[6] (1923a) 'Two Encyclopaedia Articles', S.E., Vol. 18, p. 256.
[7] (1908b) 'Character and Anal Erotism', S.E., Vol. 9, p. 45 f.
[8] (1933a) *New Introductory Lectures on Psycho-Analysis*, S.E., Vol. 22, p. 104 f.
[9] (1926d) *Inhibitions, Symptoms and Anxiety*, S.E., Vol. 20, p. 88. See also (1905d), *Three Essays on the Theory of Sexuality*, S.E., Vol. 7, p. 205 f.

expressions of sexual excitement, not only do a number of eroto-genic zones attain the significance of genitals during neuroses owing to an intensification of infantile characteristics, but the most complicated symptoms are themselves revealed as representing, by means of "conversion", phantasies which have a sexual situation as their subject-matter.'[1]

[1] (1905d) *Three Essays on the Theory of Sexuality*, S.E., Vol. 7, p. 278.

SOURCE, PRESSURE, AIM AND OBJECT OF THE SEXUAL COMPONENT INSTINCTS

(*See also: Erotogenic Zones, Component Instincts, Instincts, Aggression, Instinct and Drive, Cathexis*)

Freud first described the sexual instinct's source, aim and object in his *Three Essays on the Theory of Sexuality*, 1905, and amplified this, in the light of his developing theories, in later footnotes to the *Three Essays*, and also in 'Instincts and their Vicissitudes', 1915, and in the *New Introductory Lectures on Psycho-Analysis*, 1933.

'We can distinguish an instinct's source, object and aim. Its source is a state of excitation in the body, its aim is the removal of that excitation; on its path from its source to its aim the instinct becomes operative psychically.'[1]

In 1915 he defined instinct as 'a concept on the frontier between the mental and the somatic, as the psychical representative of the stimuli originating from within the organism and reaching the mind, as a measure of the demand made upon the mind for work, in consequence of its connection with the body'.[2]

The source

The source of an instinct is a process of excitation occurring in an organ. Excitations of two kinds arise from the somatic organs, based upon differences of a chemical nature. One of these we describe as being specifically sexual, and the organ concerned as the 'erotogenic zone' of the sexual component instinct arising from it.[3] An erotogenic zone is a part of the skin or mucous membrane in which stimuli of a certain sort evoke a feeling of pleasure possessing a particular quality. 'The character of erotogenicity can be attached to some parts of the body in a particularly marked way ... [though] any other part of the skin or mucous membrane can take over the functions of an erotogenic zone. ...' The 'satisfaction

---

[1] (1933a) *New Introductory Lectures on Psycho-Analysis*, S.E., Vol. 22, p. 96.
[2] (1915c) 'Instincts and their Vicissitudes', S.E., Vol. 14, p. 121 n.
[3] (1905d) *Three Essays on the Theory of Sexuality*, S.E., Vol. 7, p. 168.

must have been previously experienced in order to have left behind a need for its repetition'. The need for repetition of the satisfaction reveals itself in 'a peculiar feeling of tension, possessing, rather, the character of unpleasure, and by a sensation of itching or stimulation which is centrally conditioned and projected on to the peripheral erotogenic zone'.[1] Sexual excitation arises in several ways, i.e. (a) as a reproduction of a satisfaction experienced in connection with other organic processes—e.g. feeding, defecating, urination; (b) through appropriate peripheral stimulation of erotogenic zones; also as the result of various kinds of stimulation which can arouse erotogenic effects in the skin—mechanical agitation of the body, muscular activities and also intense affective processes.[2] In addition '. . . There are present in the organism contrivances which bring it about that in the case of a great number of internal processes sexual excitation arises as a concomitant effect, as soon as the intensity of those processes passes beyond certain quantitative limits. What we have called the component instincts of sexuality are either derived directly from these internal sources or are composed of elements both from those sources and from the erotogenic zones.' Individual sexual constitutions will vary according to the varying development of the erotogenic zones and of the internal sources.[3]

Freud describes how the main erotogenic zones, the oral, anal, phallic are successively stimulated because of the organic functions with which they are associated. He also says that the order in which the various instinctual impulses come into activity seems to be phylogenetically determined, so too does the length of time during which they are able to manifest themselves before they succumb to the effects of some freshly emerging instinctual impulse, or to some typical repression.[4]

Freud also stated that '. . . it may be supposed that, as a result of an appropriate stimulation of the erotogenic zones, or in other circumstances that are accompanied by an onset of sexual excitation, some substance that is disseminated generally throughout the organism becomes decomposed and the products of its decomposi-

[1] (1905d) *Three Essays on the Theory of Sexuality*, S.E., Vol. 7, p. 183 f.
[2] ibid., pp. 200–4.
[3] (1905d) *Three Essays on the Theory of Sexuality*, S.E., Vol. 7, p. 204.
[4] (1933a) *New Introductory Lectures on Psycho-Analysis*, S.E., Vol. 22, p. 98. cf. also (1905d) *Three Essays on the Theory of Sexuality*, S.E., Vol. 7, p. 241.

tion give rise to a specific stimulus which acts on the reproductive organs or upon a spinal centre related to them'.[1] (Strachey comments that it is worth noting how small a modification was made necessary in Freud's hypothesis by the discovery of sex hormones.)

The Pressure

In 'Instincts and their Vicissitudes' Freud also defines what he means by the pressure of an instinct—namely '. . . the amount of force, or the measure of the demand for work which it represents. The characteristic of exercising pressure is common to all instincts; it is in fact their very essence'.[2] An instinct 'operates as a constant force, and (is such) that the subject cannot avoid it by flight, as is possible with an external stimulus'. Every instinct is a piece of activity.[3]

The aim

Freud stated that though people 'speak of "active" and "passive" instincts', it 'would be more correct to speak of instincts with active and passive aims: for an expenditure of activity is needed to achieve a passive aim as well'. He continued: 'The aim can be achieved in the subject's own body: as a rule an external object is brought in, in regard to which the instinct achieves its external aim; its internal aim invariably remains the bodily change which is felt as satisfaction.'[4] In 'Instincts and their Vicissitudes' he again explained that the 'aim of an instinct is in every instance satisfaction, which can only be obtained by removing the state of stimulation at the source of the instinct. But although the ultimate aim of each instinct remain unchangeable, there may yet be different paths leading to the same ultimate aim; so that an instinct may be found to have various nearer or intermediate aims, which are combined or interchanged with one another'.[5]

The sexual aim of the infant is 'dominated by an erotogenic zone'.[6] It 'consists in obtaining satisfaction by means of an appropriate stimulation of the erotogenic zone . . . replacing the projected sensation of stimulation in the erotogenic zone by an external

[1] (1905d) *Three Essays on the Theory of Sexuality*, S.E., Vol. 7, p. 216 n.
[2] (1915e) 'Instincts and their Vicissitudes', S.E., Vol. 14, p. 122.
[3] (1933a) *New Introductory Lectures on Psycho-Analysis*, S.E., Vol. 22, p. 96.
[4] ibid., p. 96.
[5] (1915e) 'Instincts and their Vicissitudes', S.E., Vol. 14, p. 122.
[6] *Three Essays on Sexuality*, S.E., Vol. 7, p. 182.

stimulus which removes that sensation by producing a feeling of satisfaction'.[1]

The normal sexual aim in adults 'is regarded as being the union of the genitals in the act known as copulation, which leads to a release of the sexual tension and a temporary extinction of the sexual instinct'.[2] Freud traces the development of this mature sexual aim from infancy.

Freud describes how 'we see a great number of component instincts, arising from different areas and regions of the body, which strive for satisfaction fairly independently of one another', and how the pregenital phases of sexual life are dominated successively by the impulse to obtain satisfaction of the erotogenic zones of mouth, anus and phallus. 'These impulses which strive for pleasure are not all taken up into the final organization of the sexual function. A number of them are set aside as unserviceable, by repression or some other means; a few of them are diverted from their aim . . . and used to strengthen other impulses', then sharing their further vicissitudes.[3]

At puberty the genitalia develop into their mature form. Now, 'a new sexual aim appears, and all the component instincts combine to attain it, while the erotogenic zones become subordinated to the primacy of the genital zone . . .'.

The new sexual aim in men consists in the discharge of the sexual products, 'to which the highest degree of pleasure is attached. The sexual instinct is now subordinated to the reproductive function; it becomes, so to say, altruistic'.[4] In women the aim becomes the stimulation of the erotogenic zone of the vagina.[5]

'. . . What were formerly self-contained sexual acts, (satisfaction of erotogenic zones) attended by pleasure and excitation, become acts preparatory to the new sexual aim . . .'.[6] If 'the fore-pleasure turns out to be too great and the element of tension too small . . . the preparatory act . . . takes the place of the normal sexual aim . . . such is . . . the mechanism of many perversions'.[7] If the aims of the component instincts are repressed they may find expression as symptoms. Also what one describes as a person's character is built

---

[1] (1950a) *Three Essays on Sexuality*, S.E., Vol. 7, p. 184.
[2] (1905d) *Three Essays on the Theory of Sexuality*, S.E., Vol., 7, p. 149.
[3] (1933a) *New Introductory Lectures on Psycho-Analysis*, S.E., Vol. 22, p. 98 n.
[4] (1905d) *Three Essays on the Theory of Sexuality*, S.E., Vol. 7, p. 207.
[5] ibid., p. 221. [6] ibid., p. 234. [7] ibid., p. 211.

up to a considerable extent from the material of sexual excitations and is composed of instincts that have been fixed since childhood of constructions achieved by means of sublimation and of other constructions employed for holding in check perverse impulses which have been recognized as being unutilizable.[1] In latency the sexual aim is 'mitigated' and represents 'what may be described as the "affectionate current" of sexual life. Behind this . . . lie concealed the old sexual longings of the infantile component instincts which have now become unserviceable'.[2] This process was later termed 'inhibited in their aim'.[3]

An unpublished letter of Freud's dated 1909, makes it quite clear that he early on assumed there must be a fusion of aggression with the sexual instinct in order for the sexual aim to be achieved.

In the *New Introductory Lectures on Psycho-Analysis* after he had formulated his theory of the two fundamental instincts of Eros and aggression he describes how 'every instinctual impulse that we can examine consists of similar fusions or alloys of the two classes of instinct. These fusions, of course, would be in the most varied ratios. Thus the erotic instincts would introduce the multiplicity of their sexual aims into fusion, while the others would only admit of mitigations or gradations in their monotonous trend'.[4]

The Sexual Object
Freud uses this term both in the sense of the 'thing in regard to which or through which the instinct is able to acheive its aim' and in the sense of the love object as a whole person. In the former sense the object 'is what is most variable about an instinct and is not originally connected with it, but becomes assigned to it only in consequence of being peculiarly fitted to make satisfaction possible. The object is not necessarily something extraneous: it may equally well be a part of the subject's own body. It may be changed any number of times in the course of the vicissitudes which the instinct undergoes'.[5]

When 'the first beginnings of sexual satisfaction are still linked with the taking of nourishment, the sexual instinct has a sexual

---

[1] ibid., pp. 237–39.   [2] ibid., p. 200.
[3] (1915c) 'Instincts and Their Vicissitudes' S.E., Vol. 14, p. 122, also
   (1933a) *New Introductory Lectures on Psycho-Analysis*, S.E., Vol. 22, p. 97.
[4] (1933a) *New Introductory Lectures on Psycho-Analysis*, S.E., Vol. 22, p. 104.
[5] (1915c) 'Instincts and Their Vicissitudes', S.E., Vol. 14, p. 122.

object outside the infant's own body in the shape of his mother's breast. It is only later that the instinct loses that object . . . and becomes auto-erotic'.[1] Freud takes the example of thumb-sucking to show how 'the sexual activity, detached from the nutritive activity, has substituted for the extraneous object one situated in the subject's own body'.[2] He describes how 'infantile sexual life in spite of the preponderating influence of the erotogenic zones, exhibits components which from the very first involve other people as sexual objects. Such are the instincts of scopophilia, exhibitionism and cruelty'.[3]

In tracing the development of object love, Freud describes how the mother or nurse through their care stimulate the child's erotogenic zones and in thus 'teaching the child to love' prepare him for the choice of an object.[4]

The 'efflorescence of infantile sexual life (between the ages of two and five) already gives rise to the choice of an object, with all the wealth of mental activities which such a process involves . . . in spite of the lack of synthesis between the different instinctual components and the uncertainty of the sexual aim . . . (this phase) must be regarded as an important precursor of the subsequent final sexual organization'.[5] The onset of sexual development is interrupted by the latency period.

In puberty comes the subordination of all other sources of sexual excitation under the primacy of the genital zones and the process of finding an object . . . this is based on the child's infantile 'sexual inclination towards his parents . . . but is . . . diverted away from them, owing to the barrier against incest . . .'.[6] The infantile repressed currents and the new sensual current should converge, leading to 'the focusing of all desires upon a single object'.[7]

---

[1] (1905d) *Three Essays on the Theory of Sexuality*, S.E., Vol. 7, p. 222.
[2] ibid., p. 198.   [3] ibid., p. 191.
[4] (1905d) *Three Essays on the Theory of Sexuality*, S.E., Vol. 7, p. 222.
[5] (1905d [1920]) *Three Essays on the Theory of Sexuality*, S.E., Vol. 7, p. 234.
[6] ibid., p. 234–5.   [7] ibid., p. 200.

THE DEATH INSTINCT

Definition and Introduction

In 1938, in describing his final position as regards the theory of instincts (see: The Development of Freud's Instinct the Theory), Freud contrasted the two basic instincts, Eros and the destructive instinct. The aim of the latter 'is to undo connections and so to destroy things. We may suppose that its final aim is to lead what is living into an inorganic state. For this reason we also call it the *death instinct*. . . . In biological functions the two basic instincts operate against each other or combine with each other . . .'.

'So long as that instinct operates internally, as a death instinct, it remains silent; it only comes to our notice when it is diverted outwards as an instinct of destruction. It seems to be essential for the preservation of the individual that this diversion should occur. . . .'[1]

Throughout its development Freud's theory of the instincts remained a dualistic one (see: The Development of Freud's Instinct Theory). But it was only in 1920 that an independent destructive instinct was recognized, which then constituted one of the two basic instincts.[2] From the early days of psychoanalysis the clinical importance of aggression had been recognized, but was at first understood as a component of the sexual instinct. After 1920 aggression was understood as the manifestation of the death instinct turned outwards. In *Civilization and its Discontents*, Freud pointed out that the recognition of a special, independent aggressive instinct did not mean an alteration in the psychoanalytic theory of instincts, it merely brought into sharper focus a turn of thought arrived at long ago, whose consequences could now be followed out.[3] Though it was, of course, the problems encountered in the course of psychoanalytic experience which made it necessary to postulate the existence of the death instinct (see Concepts: The Development of Freud's Instinct Theory and Aggression), the theory of the death instinct can be discussed separately, since much

---

[1] (1940a [1938]) *An Outline of Psycho-Analysis*, S.E., Vol. 23, pp. 148–50.
[2] (1920g) *Beyond the Pleasure Principle*, S.E., Vol. 18, p. 17.
[3] (1930a) *Civilization and its Discontents*, S.E., Vol. 21, p. 117.

of Freud's reasoning is speculative and based on biological and philosophical considerations.

Theory of the Death Instinct

In *Beyond the Pleasure Principle*[1] Freud put forward the theory of the death instinct, which acts in opposition to Eros, the life instinct, comprising the sexual and self-preservative instincts, and he set out his reasoning concerning this new development in instinct theory.

He first discussed the pleasure principle—the governing tendency of the mental apparatus to avoid unpleasurable tensions by processes which lower tension.[2] He went on to point out that the repetition compulsion, as seen in dreams, the traumatic neuroses, children's play and the transference neurosis, apparently contradicts the pleasure principle; unpleasant experiences derived from the time of the oedipus complex are repeated in spite of there being no possibility of the wishes represented in them obtaining satisfaction. He said that though part of these occurrences could be understood on a rational basis, 'enough is left unexplained to justify the hypothesis of a compulsion to repeat—something that seems more primitive, more elementary, more instinctual than the pleasure principle which it over-rides . . . the pleasure principle—to which, after all, we have hitherto ascribed dominance in mental life'.[3] Following a discussion of the functions of the mental apparatus, he states that it is the task of the higher mental processes to bind instinctual excitation[4] and that only when this is accomplished can the pleasure principle proceed unhindered. The repetition compulsion in the transference neurosis and in dreams shows that the repressed memory traces have not been bound.[5]

He finally concluded that the repetition compulsion exhibits an instinctual character and stated that '. . . *An instinct is an urge inherent in organic life to restore an earlier state of things*'.[6] The death instinct aims at restoring the organism to the state of inorganic matter that existed before life arose. Freud adduced evidence from biology[7] to show that lower organisms die as a result of their own vital processes, being injured by the products of their own metabolism. But they can be rejuvenated by stimulation from without,

---

[1] (1920g) *Beyond the Pleasure Principle*, S.E., Vol. 18.
[2] ibid., pp. 7–11.   [3] ibid., pp. 17–23.   [4] ibid., p. 34.   [5] ibid., p. 36.
[6] ibid., p. 36.   [7] ibid., pp. 44–8.

that is, by the provision of fresh nutrient fluid in their environment or by conjugation with another organism (the forerunner of sexual reproduction).[1] But in these lower organisms there is as yet no differentiation between soma and germ plasm (the mortal and immortal parts).[2] It is the germ cells which work against the death of the living substance and the sexual instincts which preserve life in the species.[3] Freud applied the libido theory to the mutual relationship of cells and suggested that in multicellular organisms we may suppose that the life or sexual instincts are active in each cell, and take other cells as their object, thus partly neutralizing the death instincts, and preserving life.[4] Similarly, '. . . The life process of the individual leads for internal reasons to an abolition of chemical tensions, that is to say, to death, whereas union with the living substance of a different individual increases those tensions, introducing what may be described as fresh "vital differences" which must then be lived off. . . . The dominating tendency of mental life . . . is the effort to reduce, to keep constant or to remove internal tension due to stimuli (the nirvana principle . . .)—a tendency which finds expression in the pleasure principle; and our recognition of that fact is one of our strongest reasons for believing in the existence of death instincts.'[5] In *The Ego and the Id* he said that we must conclude that the death instincts are by their nature mute and that the clamour of life proceeds mostly from Eros and from the struggle against it. The claims of Eros introduce tensions which the id fends off in various ways. Freud noted that the condition following complete sexual satisfaction is like to dying, and that in the lower animals death coincides with copulation because, after satisfaction has eliminated Eros, the death instinct has a free hand.[6]

Freud said that though there had been ample opportunity to study the libidinal instincts, the analysis of the ego had not yet proceeded far enough to allow of the study of other instincts.[7] However, there is a parallel to the opposition of the life and death instincts in the love-hate polarity. Further, the sadistic component of the sexual instinct has long been recognized, and if the libidinal and self-preservative instincts are now to be subsumed under Eros, this sadistic instinct, whose aim is to injure the object, can scarcely

[1] ibid., p. 48.   [2] ibid., p. 49.   [3] ibid., p. 40.   [4] ibid., p. 50.
[5] ibid., pp. 55–6.   [6] (1923b) *The Ego and the Id*, S.E., Vol. 19, pp. 46–7.
[7] (1920g) *Beyond the Pleasure Principle*, S.E., Vol. 18, p. 53.

be derived from Eros, the preserver of life. Consequently, Freud concluded that sadism is a death instinct, which, under the influence of narcissism, has been forced away from the ego and has emerged in relation to the object.[1] If there is no difference in principle between an instinct turning from an object to the ego, and its turning from the ego to an object, masochism would be a regression to an earlier phase of the instinct's history, so that there might be such a thing as primary masochism, a proposition hitherto rejected.[2] This question was taken up again in 'The Economic Problem of Masochism' where Freud stated that in multicellular organisms the libido has the task of making the destroying instinct innocuous, which it does by diverting that instinct outwards, as the destructive instinct, the instinct for mastery or the will to power, and by means of *fusion*.[3] A portion of the instinct is placed directly in the service of the sexual function—sadism proper[4] part remains operative within the organism—primal sadism, identical with masochism. Erotogenic masochism, which has also become a component of the libido, is a remainder from the phase of development in which coalescence between Eros and the death instinct took place.[5] (This question is fully discussed under *Sadism* and *Masochism*.)

Libidinal regression results in the setting free of the previously bound instinct of destruction, directed towards the object. This occurs in obsessional neurosis, and then the ego has to defend against the anal-sadistic impulses.[6] The released impulses add to the severity of the super-ego.[7] In melancholia, where the ego identifies with the lost object and the libido regresses to narcissism, all the destructive impulses, now entrenched in the super-ego, are turned against the ego. 'A pure culture of the death instinct' holds sway in the super-ego, hence the tendency to suicide.[8]

[1] (1920) *Beyond the Pleasure Principle*, S.E., Vol. 18, pp. 53–4.
[2] ibid., pp. 54–5.
[3] (1924c) 'The Economic Problem of Masochism', S.E., Vol. 19, pp. 163–4.
[4] ibid., p. 163.   [5] ibid., p. 164.
[6] (1923b) *The Ego and the Id.*, S.E., Vol. 19, p. 53.
[7] ibid., p. 55.   [8] ibid., p. 53.

THE AGGRESSIVE DRIVE

The concept of aggression cannot be studied in isolation. Its development has been dependent on developments in the libido theory, without which it cannot be understood. The development of instinct theory falls into four phases, the first and last subdivided and Freud's understanding of aggression and its origin changes accordingly. (See Concept: The Development of Freud's Instinct Theory.)

Phases 1 and 2
From the early days of psychoanalysis Freud recognized the clinical importance of the individual's aggressive impulses towards external objects. But at the time when he classified instincts in the two categories, sexual and self-preservative, aggressive impulses were regarded as sadistic components of the sexual instinct. Even in *Three Essays on the Theory of Sexuality* (1905d) Freud was not satisfied with this explanation of the origin of aggression, and in 1909 he suggested that both the sexual and self-preservative instincts had the power of becoming aggressive. The aggressive component of instincts was seen as being in some way related to the need to obtain mastery over the external world.

Phase 3
In 'Instincts and their Vicissitudes' (1915c), Freud reached the conclusion that aggression could not be classified as a libidinal impulse, and suggested that it originated in the self-preservative instincts.

Phase 4a
In *Beyond the Pleasure Principle* (1920g), when Freud reclassified the instincts, both sexual and self-preservative instincts were subsumed under the life instinct, and aggression was no longer considered to originate in the self-preservative instincts, but was now seen as the outward directed manifestation of the death instinct. Freud emphasized that aggression could only be studied

71

as it occurred mixed with libido, so that the concepts of *fusion and defusion* became important.

The essential importance of his postulation of the *Death Instinct* was not, therefore, the recognition of the part played by aggression in human psychopathology, but the new metapsychological understanding it gave of the origins and vicissitudes of the aggressive or destructive tendencies. This led, of course, to new insights into clinical problems. Freud was led to reverse his former opinion that sadism was primary to masochism.

Phase 4b
After *The Ego and the Id* (1923b), with the introduction of structural concepts the new conception of aggression was particularly important for the understanding of obsessional neurosis and melancholia, since it threw new light on the process of super-ego formation.

HISTORICAL DEVELOPMENT OF FREUD'S
THINKING ON AGGRESSION

Phase 1 and 2
Freud was already giving passing thought to the problem of sexual aggression before the turn of the century. He presumably concurred with the view expressed by Breuer in *Studies on Hysteria* (1895d), that an increase of sexual excitation in male animals leads to an intensification of the aggressive instinct;[1] and that in normal and healthy young men sexuality is 'an unmixed aggressive instinct'.[2]

It seems that at this time Freud was considering only manifest aggression directed outwards, and that he linked aggression with activity and masculinity, sexual aggressiveness being a male prerogative, while feminine development was considered to be passive from the start. (This, of course, was prior to his investigation of the similarities and differences between masculine and feminine development, and the relationship between *passivity–activity* and *masculinity–femininity* (see those concepts). For example, according to his understanding of the aetiology of the neuroses at that time, he thought in the aetiology of obsessional neurosis there was to be found for men 'an act of aggression

[1] (1895d) With Breuer, *Studies on Hysteria*, S.E., Vol. 2, pp. 200–1.
[2] ibid., p. 246.

inspired by desire', whereas for women there was to be found only 'a participation in sexual relations accompanied by enjoyment'.[1] At this time he thought that acts of sexual aggressiveness in children could not occur without a previous seduction.[2]

He gave a more detailed exposition of his views in *Three Essays on the Theory of Sexuality* (1905d), thought his main concern here was not to understand aggression *per se*, but to understand sadism. He said that male sexuality contains an element of aggressiveness— the desire to subjugate—because of the need to overcome the resistance of the sexual object. The perversion of sadism 'would correspond to an aggressive component of the sexual instinct which has become independent and exaggerated and, by displacement, has usurped the leading position'[3] (see Concepts: Sadism and Masochism).

Freud was not satisfied with the available explanations of sadism or aggressiveness at this time. He said that nothing had been done towards explaining the intimate connection between cruelty (sadism) and the sexual instinct 'apart from laying emphasis on the aggressive factor in the libido. According to some authorities this aggressive element of the sexual instinct is in reality a relic of cannibalistic desires—that is, it is a contribution derived from the apparatus for obtaining mastery, which is concerned with the satisfaction of the other and, ontogenetically, the older of the great instinctual needs'.[4] In *Jokes and their Relation to the Unconscious* (1905c), there is a passage in which Freud appears to differentiate between aggressiveness, in the sense of the desire to subjugate or master, and sadism, though both are considered to be libidinal impulses. He is speaking of what happens when the man's sexual aggressiveness (as expressed in sexually exciting speech) is faced with an obstacle, and therefore alters its character. 'It becomes positively hostile and cruel, and it thus summons to its help against the obstacle the sadistic components of the sexual instinct.'[5] However, in other contexts (in 1905c) this differentiation is not made.

---

[1] (1896a) 'Heredity and the Aetiology of the Neuroses', S.E., Vol. 3, pp. 155–6.
[2] ibid., p. 155 (cf. also (1896c) 'The Aetiology of Hysteria', S.E., Vol. 3, p. 208).
[3] (1905d) *Three Essays on theTheory of Sexuality*, S.E., Vol. 7, pp. 157–8.
[4] ibid., p. 159.
[5] (1905c) *Jokes and their Relation to the Unconscious*, S.E., Vol. 8, p. 99.

In the passages mentioned above, aggression is considered to be a libidinal impulse. But in the 1905d edition of the *Three Essays* there was a passage, deleted in later editions in which Freud suggested that 'the impulse of cruelty' (referring to the sadistic impulse) might arise from sources independent of sexuality, though this would seem to foreshadow the final development of Freud's theory of instincts the two become united at an early stage (see The Development of Freud's Instinct Theory).[1]

Freud then remained for many years unwilling to accept the existence of an independent instinct of aggression. In 1909b, in the course of his discussion of the hostile and aggressive propensities of 'Little Hans', he stated strongly his disagreement with Adler's concept of an aggressive instinct, saying that he preferred to adhere to the view that each instinct (sexual and self-preservative) has its own power of becoming aggressive. Thus here, aggression is no longer thought of simply as a libidinal impulse.[2]

Phase 3

The next step in Freud's investigation of the origins of aggression came in 1915c, when he rejected the notion that aggression is a libidinal impulse. In 'Instincts and their Vicissitudes' (1915c) he discusses the polarity of love (affection) and hate (aggressiveness) which he was later to compare with the polarity between the life and death instincts, and he recognizes the complexity of the relationship between love and hate.[3] He states that hate is older than love, it arises from a different, i.e. non-libidinal source, and he suggests that this source is the self-preservative instincts.[4] Hate was originally the ego's reaction to the external world with its unwelcome influx of stimuli,[5] so that in the course of their development 'the sexual and ego-instincts can readily develop an antithesis which repeats that of love and hate'[6] (see also Ambivalence). However, as a result of his work on narcissism, Freud was already questioning in this paper whether the distinction between the libidinal (object) instincts and the self-preservative (ego) instincts could be upheld any longer[7] (see Concept: The Development of Freud's Instinct Theory). Indeed, in an addition to the *Three*

---

[1] (1905d) *Three Essays on the Theory of Sexuality*, S.E., Vol. 7, p. 193 n.

[2] (1909b) 'Analysis of a Phobia in a Five-Year-Old Boy', S.E., Vol. 10, pp. 140–1.

[3] (1915c) 'Instincts and their Vicissitudes', S.E., Vol. 14, p. 138.

[4] ibid., p. 139.   [5] ibid., p. 137.   [6] ibid., p. 139.   [7] ibid., p. 124.

Essays made in the same year, he remarked that the origins of aggression were not yet understood.[1]

The new understanding of the way in which hostile, destructive tendencies, originally directed to external objects, are turned back on the self in melancholia [(1917e [1915]) ('Mourning and Melancholia', S.E., Vol. 14)], made it difficult to uphold for long the view that aggression has its origins in the self-preservative instincts, for aggression could no longer be explained simply as the impulse to mastery over the external world. (See Concept: The Development of Freud's Instinct Theory.)

Phase 4a

The next step came in 1920g, when, with a drastic revision of this theory, Freud subsumed both sexual and self-preservative instincts under Eros—the life instinct—and postulated the existence of the death instinct, in opposition to Eros (see concept: the death instinct). Aggression was now no longer considered to have its origins in the self-preservative instincts, but in the death instinct, and Freud compared the polarity of love (affection) and hate (aggressiveness) with the polarity of the life and death instincts.[2] In *Beyond the Pleasure Principle* Freud was mainly concerned with the workings of the death instinct within the organism, but in later papers he turned his attention to the way in which the death instincts are directed outwards, becoming manifest as destructive or aggressive impulses. He stated that the erotic and death instincts are present only in varying mixtures or fusions though defusion can occur under certain circumstances.[3] This topic is pursued in *The Ego and the Id* (1923b) where he states that the concept of fusion is an indispensable assumption. The death instinct expresses itself partly as an instinct of destruction directed against the external world and other organisms, and for purposes of discharge is habitually brought into the service of Eros. 'The sadistic component of the sexual instinct would be a classical example of a serviceable instinctual fusion; and the sadism which has made itself independent as a perversion would be typical of a defusion, though not of one carried to extremes'[4] (see Concepts: Fusion-Defusion, Sadism).

[1] (1905d) *Three Essays on the Theory of Sexuality*, S.E., Vol. 7, pp. 159, and 200-1.

[2] (1920g) *Beyond the Pleasure Principle*, S.E., Vol. 18, p. 53.

[3] (1923a [1922]) 'Two Encyclopedia Articles', S.E., Vol. 18, p. 258.

[4] (1923b) *The Ego and the Id*, S.E., Vol. 19, p. 41.

Phase 4b

Shortly after his 1920g formulation of instinct theory, Freud introduced his structural concepts in 1923b (see concept: The Development of Freud's Instinct Theory) and the new formulations concerning aggression allowed of new understanding of the process of super-ego formation. When the super-ego is set up it is endowed with that part of the child's aggressiveness which, because of his love for them, he cannot direct against the parents, who frustrate his instinctual wishes. The internalized parents become the super-ego, but the severity of the super-ego corresponds not with the severity of the parents, but with the amount of the child's aggressiveness towards them, now taken into the super-ego).[1] The identifications and introjections occurring in super-ego formation involve an instinctual defusion, so that the released destructive impulses add to the severity of the super-ego)[2] (see Concepts: Fusion-Defusion).

Libidinal regression also results in the setting free of the previously bound instinct of destruction, directed towards the object. This occurs in obsessional neurosis, and the ego has to defend against the anal-sadistic impulses.[3] In melancholia, where the ego identifies with the lost object and the libido regresses to narcissism, all the destructive impulses, now entrenched in the supergo, are turned against the own ego. 'A pure culture of the death instinct holds sway in the super-ego', hence the tendency to suicide.[4]

In *Civilization and its Discontents* (1930a), Freud noted that the analytic literature shows a predilection for the idea that any kind of frustration results in a heightening of the sense of guilt. But he says that this should be regarded as applying only to the aggressive instincts, since we cannot account on dynamic and economic grounds for an increase in the sense of guilt appearing in place of unfulfilled erotic demands. 'When an instinctual trend undergoes repression, its libidinal elements are turned into symptoms, and its aggressive component into a sense of guilt.'[5]

---

[1] (1930a) *Civilization and its Discontents*, S.E., Vol. 21, pp. 129–30.

[2] (1923b) *The Ego and the Id*, S.E., Vol. 19, pp. 54–5; cf. also (1924c) 'The Economic Problem of Masochism', S.E., Vol. 19, p. 167.

[3] (1923b) *The Ego and the Id.*, S.E., Vol. 19, p. 53.

[4] ibid., p. 53.

[5] (1930a) *Civilization and its Discontents*, S.E., Vol. 21, pp. 138–9.

CLINICAL APPLICATIONS

The changes in understanding of clinical problems as a result of the development of Freud's ideas about aggression were mainly related to the understanding of the super-ego.

The Negative Therapeutic Reaction

Following the introduction of the death instinct, the negative therapeutic reaction was understood as one of the results of defusion and the taking over of aggressive impulses by the super-ego, leading to the need for punishment on the part of the ego, so that the patient reacts adversely to improvements during his treatment.[1]

Melancholia

In (1917d[1915]) 'Mourning and Melancholia', the self-reproaches and self-torment of the melancholiac were recognized as emanating from the super-ego—at that time referred to as 'conscience', 'a critical institution in the mind, split off from the ego',[2] and directed against the own ego because of its identification with the lost object.[3] The self-torment signifies a gratification of sadistic impulses and of hate, and the illness develops as a means of avoiding the open expression of hostility to the love object.[4]

In *The Ego and the Id* (1923b) the 'conscience' became the super-ego and its severity towards the ego could be explained in terms of defusion and the taking into the super-ego of the destructive instincts.[5] The ego gives up itself because it feels hated and persecuted by the super-ego. Living means being loved by the super-ego.[6]

Obsessional Neurosis

The study of aggression in obsessional neurosis has a long history. In 1896c, 'The Aetiology of Hysteria', Freud said that obsessions can be shown by analysis to be disguised and transformed self-reproaches about acts of sexual aggression in childhood.[7] The role played by repressed sadistic and hostile impulses and the importance of ambivalence were recognized and these were understood as

[1] (1933a) *New Introductory Lectures on Psycho-Analysis*, S.E., Vol. 22, pp. 109–10.
[2] (1917d [1915]) 'Mourning and Melancholia', S.E., Vol. 14, p. 247.
[3] ibid., p. 249.   [4] ibid., p. 251.
[5] (1923b) *The Ego and the Id.*, S.E., Vol. 19, pp. 53–4.   [6] ibid., p. 58.
[7] (1896c) 'The Aetiology of Hysteria', S.E., Vol. 2, p. 220.

leading to the conflict represented in the obsessional symptoms.[1] In 'The Disposition to Obsessional Neurosis' (1913i) Freud put forward the suggestion that a precocity of ego development, necessitating a choice of object under the influence of the ego instincts at a time when the sexual instinct was still in the pre-genital stage, might be included in the disposition to obsessional neurosis. Since, 'in the order of development, hate is the precursor of love', such a precocity might account for the obsessional's need to develop a super-morality in order to protect his love object.[2]

Following the introduction of structural concepts and of the destructive instinct, Freud reformulated these views, and related the severity of the super-ego in obsessional neurosis to the regression of libido to the sadistic anal stage, accompanied by instinctual defusion, and the taking in of destructive impulses into the super-ego.[3]

SOCIOLOGICAL CONSIDERATIONS

After 1920 Freud gave considerable attention to the role of the destructive instinct in group formation and civilization. The most detailed exposition is to be found in *Civilization and its Discontents* (1930a), where he states that a powerful share of aggressiveness must be reckoned among the instinctual endowments of man, so that a neighbour 'is not only a potential helper or sexual object, but also someone who tempts them to satisfy their aggressiveness on him'.[4]

As a rule this aggressiveness only appears under provocation, or puts itself at the service of some other purpose. But in favourable circumstances man can reveal himself as 'a savage beast to whom consideration toward his own kind is something alien'. 'In consequence of this primary mutual hostility of human beings civilized society is perpetually threatened with disintegration.'[5]

In civilization manifestations of aggressiveness are checked by means of identifications, aim-inhibited love relationships, restriction on sexual life and reaction formations.[6] A small group

---

[1] (1909d) 'Notes Upon a Case of Obsessional Neurosis', S.E., Vol. 10, pp. 192 and 240–1.

[2] (1913i) 'The Disposition to Obsessional Neurosis,' S.E., Vol. 12, p. 325.

[3] (1926d) *Inhibitions, Symptoms and Anxiety*, S.E., Vol. 20, p. 113.

[4] (1930a) *Civilization and its Discontents*, S.E., Vol. 21, p. 111.

[5] ibid., pp. 111–12.   [6] ibid., p. 112.

allows an outlet for aggression in the form of hostility to outsiders.[1] In return for the sacrifices imposed on his sexuality and aggression, civilized man gains more security.[2]

Civilization is a process in the service of Eros, whose purpose is to combine individuals into ever larger units. But man's natural aggressive instinct, the derivative and main representative of the death instinct, opposes this programme of civilization. The evolution of civilization presents the struggle between Eros and the death instinct as it works itself out in the human species.[3] The most important method of dealing with aggression is its internalization and taking over by the super-ego of the role of the authorities who frustrate instinctual wishes.

[1] ibid., p. 114.   [2] ibid., p. 115.   [3] ibid., p. 122.

FUSION–DEFUSION

Historical Considerations

Fusion and defusion are energic, instinctual concepts. Their importance derives from the fact that psychoanalysis has worked with a dual instinct theory. These terms describe the degree to which instincts are found in combination with each other. Freud used a number of terms to describe the inter-mixing of instincts (including alloying, amalgamation, coalescence) and I will return to this later. For the purposes of this paper, the terms *fusion* and *defusion* will be used in the general sense, to refer to the general process.

In Freud's earlier instinct theory (the dual instincts of the libido and the ego) one sees a precursor of 'fusion' in the term 'confluence':

'We suspect that instincts other than those of self-preservation operate in the ego, and it ought to be possible for us to point to them. Unfortunately, however, the analysis of the ego has made so little headway that it is very difficult for us to do so. (In the first edition only, this quotation continued.) It is possible, indeed, that the libidinal instincts in the ego may be linked in a peculiar manner . . . by instinctual "confluence", to borrow a term used by Adler (1908) . . . with these other ego instincts which are still strange to us.'[1]

With the study of narcissistic disorders, it had become apparent that the theoretical separation-distinction of ego and sexual instincts could not be logically maintained. Yet clinical evidence was clear that some distinction existed. Freud's arguments in 1916/17, in the *Introductory Lectures on Psycho-Analysis*, clearly states the necessity of making the distinction between sexual and other instincts. His other comments, in this context, reflect the general problem of working with psychological concepts that have their origins in biology:

[1] (1920g) *Beyond the Pleasure Principle*, S.E., Vol. 18, p. 53, n. 2.

'Our right to separate the ego-instincts from the sexual ones cannot, no doubt, be shaken; it is implied in the existence of sexual life as a distinct activity of the individual. The only question is what importance we attribute to this separation, how deep-going we wish to consider it. The answer to this question, however, will be guided by how far we are able to establish the extent to which the sexual instincts behave differently in their somatic and mental manifestations from the others which we are contrasting with them, and how important the consequences are which arise from those differences. Moreover, we have, of course, no motive for asserting an essential difference between the two groups of instincts which is not plainly appreciable. Both of them come before us merely as designations of sources of energy in the individual, and the discussion as to whether they are fundamentally one or essentially different and as to when, if they are one, they became separate from each other—this discussion cannot be conducted on the basis of the connotation of the terms but must keep to the biological facts lying behind them. At the moment we know too little about these, and even if we knew more it would have no relevance for our analytic task.

'It is obvious, too, that we shall profit very little if, following Jung's example, we insist upon the original unity of all the instincts and give the name of "libido" to the energy manifested in all of them. Since no device whatever will make it possible to eliminate the sexual function from mental life, we shall in that case find ourselves obliged to speak of sexual and asexual libido.'[1]

In semi-autobiographical comment in *Civilization and Its Discontents* (1930a) Freud noted the problems that evolved from the older instinct theory and the theoretical solution that followed his proposal of the death and life instincts:

'. . . It seemed for a time inevitable that we should make libido coincide with instinctual energy in general, as C. G. Jung had already advocated earlier. Nevertheless, there still remained in me a kind of conviction . . . that the instincts could not all be of the same kind.'[2]

---

[1] (1916–17) *Introductory Lectures on Psycho-Analysis*, S.E., Vol. 16, pp. 412–3.
[2] (1930a) *Civilization and its Discontents*, S.E., Vol. 21, p. 118.

Besides the narcissistic disorders, the problems of sadism and masochism were not easily accounted for by the theory of the libido. Again, in another apparent reminiscence, Freud noted that it was 'only proper if what was a stumbling-block for the one theory should become the corner-stone of the theory replacing it'.[1] While the narcissistic disorders showed the limitations of the earlier libido theory, masochism and sadism pointed towards the concepts of fusions and defusions of the primal life and death instincts.

Genetic formulations

Freud has commented elsewhere that the instinct theory lay on the borderland of biology. It is not surprising to find that his formulations as to fusion of the instincts also use a biological model. Freud hypothesized in *The Ego and the Id*:

'On this view, a special physiological process (of anabolism or catabolism) would be associated with each of the two classes of instincts; both kinds of instinct would be active in every particle of living substance, though in unequal proportions, so that some one substance might be the principal representative of Eros.'[2]

Freud essentially reaffirmed this biological view, or analogy, throughout his work and as late as *An Outline of Psycho-Analysis* (1940a[1938]), he notes:

'Within this id the organic *instincts* operate, which are themselves compounded of fusions of two primal forces (Eros and destructiveness) in varying proportions and are differentiated from one another by their relation to organs or systems of organs.'[3]

This seems to be more than a 'biological model' which is only used to provide an analogy for psychological processes. Rather Freud seems to clearly infer that fusion takes place at a biological level:

'It appears that, as a result of the combination of unicellular organisms into multicellular forms of life, the death instinct of the

---

[1] (1933a) *New Introductory Lectures on Psycho-Analysis*, S.E., Vol. 22, p. 104.

[2] (1923b) *The Ego and the Id*, S.E., Vol. 19, p. 41.

[3] (1940a[1938]) *An Outline of Psycho-Analysis*, S.E., Vol. 23, pp. 197-8.

single cell can successfully be neutralized and the destructive impulses be diverted on to the external world. . . .'[1]

While Freud is not explicit, he seems to equate the tendency towards fusion/binding with the life instincts and the tendency towards defusion/disintegration to the death instincts:

'The aim of the first of these basic instincts is to establish ever greater unities and to preserve them thus . . . in short, to bind together; the aim of the second is, on the contrary, is to undo connections and to destroy things. We may suppose that the final aim of the destructive instinct is to reduce living things to an inorganic state. For this reason we also call it the *death instinct*.

'We may picture an initial state of things by supposing that the whole available energy of Eros, to which we shall hence-forward give the name of 'libido', is present in the still undifferentiated ego-id and serves to neutralize the destructive impulses which are simultaneously present.'[2]

Where Freud refers to the primal instincts of life and death, and the organic nature of fusions, one is impressed that his formulations are biological concepts, and as such might be distinguished from the equivalent or parallel processes which are of a psychological nature. As Freud has clearly stated elsewhere, the instincts can not be experienced or known directly but only through their derivatives, through the medium of the ego. Where Freud moves on to speak of 'aggression' in the 'id', he seems to have made the clear step from a biological to a psychological model.

Binding and Neutralization
Since it will be necessary to comment on the relationship of the concept of fusion-defusion to the *concepts* of binding and neutralization, it seems desirable to note a terminological complication that can give rise to confusion. Freud also uses the terms *bound* and *neutralized* in a seemingly descriptive way when referring to the life instinct:

[1] (1923b) *The Ego and the Id*, S.E., Vol. 19, p. 41.
[2] (1940a[1938]) *An Outline of Psycho-Analysis*, S.E., Vol. 23, pp. 149–50.

'. . . The death instinct of the single cell can successfully be neutralised . . .'

'. . . The main purpose of Eros . . . that of uniting and binding . . .'[1]

'How large the portions of the death instincts are which refuse to be tamed in this way by being bound to admixtures of libido we cannot at present guess.'[2]

'The aim of the first of these basic instincts is to establish ever greater unities and to preserve them thus, in short, to bind together . . . the total available energy of Eros . . . serves to neutralize the destructive tendencies which are simultaneously present.'[3]

This use of terms seems clearly descriptive, to portray the characteristics of the instincts. The concept of binding refers to a different process, to the inhibition of mobile cathexes. Neutralization, as a concept, refers to the modification/the transformation, of libidinal energies into desexualized, neutralized energy.

Towards a definition
In different papers and at different times, Freud used various expressions and descriptions to refer to the mixing or combining of instincts. In the English translations, *fusion* and *defusion* are the best-known terms, but Freud used a number of other expressions which may add to our understanding of his meaning: 'instinctual confluence' (*Beyond the Pleasure Principle*, 1920g, p. 53.); 'regular mixtures' ('Two Encyclopedia Articles', 1923a, pp. 258–9); 'fused, blended and alloyed', 'aggressiveness which was mixed with libido' (*The Ego and the Id*, 1923b, pp. 41 and 55); 'the taming of the death-instinct by the libido', 'extensive fusion and amalgamation, in varying proportions', 'mixtures of them in different amounts', 'coalescence between death instinct and Eros', ('The Economic Problems of Masochism', 1924c, p. 164); 'alloyed with each other in varying and very different proportions' (*Civilization and its Discontents*, 1930a, pp. 118–19); 'it is always accompanied

---

[1] (1923b) *The Ego and the Id*, S.E., Vol. 19, pp. 41 and 45.
[2] (1924c) 'The Economic Problem of Masochism', S.E., Vol. 19, p. 164.
[3] (1940a [1938]) *An Outline of Psycho-Analysis*, S.E., Vol. 23, pp. 148–50.

. . . or, as we say, alloyed . . . with an element from the other side, which modifies its aim or is, in some cases, what enables it to achieve that aim' (*Why War?* 1933b, p. 209). We know that Freud had once considered the transformation of instincts into their opposites and he discussed this at length in the *The Ego and the Id* pp. 44–7) where he discarded the idea. (This was the argument in which he introduced the hypothesis of desexualized, neutral energies transformed from libido.)

In the German, Freud seems no more explicit: e.g. '*eine Trie-bentmischung*', '*dieser Entmischung*'; '*mit eingehender verbinden*', '*vermischen*', '*legieren*' (G.W. 13, pp. 284–5 and 269). The ambiguity seems more to stem from the nature of the phenomenon and the difficulty in assessing it. As late as 1933a, Freud commented that how the two instincts are 'mingled in the process of living, how the death instinct is made to serve the purposes of Eros . . . these are tasks which are left to future investigation'.[1]

The general dictionary meaning of the term 'fusion' seems quite consistent with Freud's meaning of alloying and mixing. But contemporary physics and chemistry denote *fusion* in a different way, *viz.* the union of two elements (compounds) into a third element (compound) with different characteristics from either of the original elements.

Freud's 'meaning' of fusion seems clearest in his descriptive comments:

'Neither of these instincts is any less essential than the other; the phenomena of life arise from the concurrent or mutually opposing action of both. Now it seems as though an instinct of the one sort can scarcely ever operate in isolation; it is always accompanied—or, as we say, alloyed—with a certain quota from the other side, which modifies its aim or is, in some cases, what enables it to achieve that aim. Thus, for instance, the instinct of self-preservation is certainly of an erotic kind, but it must nevertheless have aggressiveness at its disposal if it is to fulfill its purpose. So, too, the instinct of love, when it is directed towards an object, stands in need of some contribution from the instinct for mastery if it is in any way to obtain possession of that object.'[2]

---

[1] (1933a) *New Introductory Lectures on Psycho-Analysis*, S.E., Vol. 22, p. 107.
[2] (1933b) *Why War?* S.E., Vol. 22, pp. 209–10.

'Modifications in the proportions of the fusion between the instincts have the most tangible results. A surplus of sexual aggressiveness will turn a lover into a sex murderer, while a sharp diminution in the aggressive factor will make him bashful or impotent.'[1]

From this I assume that Freud considered that both libidinal and aggressive cathexes are simultaneous with regard to an object and that the quality of the aggression or love that may be expressed will depend on the relative strength of each. The 'fusion' consists in the combination of the drives in differing, relative proportions.

Miss Freud's formulations seem to support this view:

'. . . the love—and hate—reactions of human beings are inter-mixed by nature, and from the beginning of object relationships in the life of the individual, both opposing tendencies are directed towards the same persons. This implies that the infant develops hostile as well as loving feelings toward the mother.

'Further in infants, love and hate, affection and anger, tenderness and aggression, the wish to destroy loved people or toys and the wish to preserve and have them, can be seen to appear in quick succession seemingly unaffected by each other, each controversial striving attempting with full force to reach its own aim. The mental representative of the two organic forces remain unrelated to each other so long as no central point or awareness is established in the personality. It is only the growth of this focal point (the ego) which results in the gradual integration of all instinctive strivings, and during this process, may lead to clashes and realization of incompatibility between them.'[2]

The balance of fused libidinal and aggressive energies has yet another vicissitude and can be modified by means other than the proportion of the instinctual drives. In his formulations on neutralized energies, Freud noted that 'displaceable energy, which, neutral in itself, can be added to a qualitatively differentiated erotic or destructive impulse and augment its total cathexis'.[3]

---

[1] (1940a [1938]) *An Outline of Psycho-Analysis*, S.E., Vol. 23, p. 149.

[2] (1949) Freud, A., 'Notes on Aggression', *Bulletin of the Menninger Clinic*, pp. 147 and 149.

[3] (1923b) *The Ego and the Id*, S.E., Vol. 19, p. 41.

The indefiniteness of Freud's formulations may derive from his conviction that too little was known about the process; as late as 1933, Freud remained uncertain:

'We recognize two basic instincts and give each of them its own aim. How the two of them are mingled in the process of living, how the death instinct is made to serve the purposes of Eros, especially by being turned outwards as aggressiveness—these are tasks which are left to future investigation.'[1]

Structural formulations
Fused or partially defused energies are used by the ego and super-ego, as well as neutral energies. It is clear that Freud considered that all structures of the mind used such energies:

'Here we are dealing with the ultimate things which psychological research can learn about: the behaviour of the two primal instincts, their distribution mingling and defusion things which we cannot think of as being confined to a single province of the mental apparatus, the id, the ego or the super-ego.'[2]

With the narcissistic cathexis of ego functions, and the self, Freud hypothesizes that libidinal energies are used because of the libido's innate tendency for binding and drawing together. But the process of neutralization, desexualization, of libido implies that aggressive energies will be simultaneously defused.

'I cannot go further in my consideration of these questions without introducing a fresh hypothesis. The super-ego arises, as we know, from an identification with the father taken as a model. Every such identification is in the nature of a desexualization or even of a sublimation. It now seems as though when a transformation of this kind takes place, an instinctual defusion occurs at the same time. After sublimation the erotic component no longer has the power to bind the whole of the destructiveness that was combined with it, and this is released in the form of an inclination to aggression and destruction. This defusion would be the source of the

---

[1] (1933a) *New Introductory Lectures on Psycho-Analysis*, S.E., Vol. 22, p. 107.
[2] (1937c) 'Analysis Terminable and Interminable', S.E., Vol. 23, p. 242.

general character of harshness and cruelty exhibited by the ideal
. . . its dictatorial "Thou shalt".'[1]

In this view, the very process of neutralization is a potential
danger since the release of defused aggression might be turned
against the self. (But see Hartmann, 'Notes on the Theory of
Sublimation', *The Psychoanalytic Study of the Child*, Vol. X, 1955,
for an alternative formulation in which defused aggression would
be used by the ego for the energies of defence.)

Clinical Implications

The concepts of fusion and defusion proves helpful in considering
a wide range of phenomena. Indeed, as would be expected from
the fact that the concepts relate to the basic instincts, fusion and
defusion should be ascertainable in all aspects of normal and
pathological behaviour.

'The instinct of destruction, moderated and tamed, and as it were,
inhibited in its aim, must, when it is directed towards objects,
provide the ego with the satisfaction of its vital needs and with
control over nature.'[2]

'But we must not be too hasty in introducing ethical judgements of
good and evil. Neither of these instincts is any less essential than
the other; the phenomena of life arise from the concurrent or
mutually opposing of both. Now it seems as though an instinct of
the one sort can scarcely ever operate in isolation; it is always
accompanied—or, as we say, alloyed—with a certain quota from
the other side. . . .'[3]

It is the aggressive component, via fusion, that gives the motive/
drive force to the libidinal impulse. And it is the libidinal characteristic that helps to check or divert the discharge of the aggressive
impulse. Freud alludes to the qualitative distinction in the 'mixture', *viz.* that '. . . the erotic instincts would introduce the
multiplicity of their sexual aims into the fusion, while the others
would only admit of mitigations or gradations in their monotonous
trend. . . .'[4]

[1] (1923b) *The Ego and the Id*, S.E., Vol. 19, pp. 54–5.
[2] (1930a) *Civilization and its Discontents*, S.E., Vol. 21, pp. 121–2.
[3] (1933b) *Why War ?* S.E., Vol. 22, p. 209.
[4] (1933a) *New Introductory Lectures on Psycho-Analysis*, S.E., Vol. 22, p. 105.

Identification and sublimation are processes involving the desexualization of libido, with the consequent defusion of aggression. The inherent consequence of identification and sublimation is thus the 'liberation of aggressive instincts in the super-ego, (and) its struggle against the libido exposes it to the anger of maltreatment and death'.[1]

Regression

'Making a swift generalization, we might conjecture that the essence of a regression of libido (e.g. from the genital to the sadistic-anal phase) lies in a defusion of instincts, just as, conversely, the advance from the earlier phase to the definitive genital one would be conditioned by an accession of erotic components.'[2]

This suggests that Freud saw advance in libidinal phases of development as contributing to an increase in capacity for fusion. The reverse process of regression would involve a defusion via the return to early forms of instinctual discharge, again with the possible consequence of an increase in aggression turned against the self:

'Perhaps regression is the result not of a constitutional factor but of a time factor. It may be that regression is rendered possible not because the genital organization of the libido is too feeble but because the opposition of the ego begins too early, while the sadistic phase is at its heights.

'As regards the metapsychological explanation of regression, I am inclined to find it in a "defusion of instinct", in a detachment of the erotic components which, with the onset of the genital stage, had joined the destructive cathexis belonging to the sadistic phase.'[3]

Guilt and symptom formation were also related theoretically to defusion with (1) the libidinal elements of the repressed instinctual trend being turned into symptoms and (2) the aggression turned into a sense of guilt. 'Even if this proposition is only an average approximation to the truth, it is worthy of our interest.'[4]

---

[1] (1923b) *The Ego and the Id*, S.E., Vol. 19, pp. 56–7. [2] ibid., p. 42.
[3] (1926d) *Inhibitions, Symptoms and Anxiety*, S.E., Vol. 20, pp. 113–14.
[4] (1930a) *Civilization and its Discontents*, S.E., Vol. 21, p. 139.

Both *primary and secondary masochism* can be adduced from the formulations of fusion and defusion. Freud approached this problem in 'The Economic Problem of Masochism', 1924c, where he hypothesized simultaneous differentiation of drives and differentiation of self from the object world (p. 164). In the stage of narcissism, the self was the sole object of drive discharge when aggressive, destructive drives were restrained only by their instinctual fusion. With the 'transposition' outwards of the death instinct, some residual aggression, fused with libido, would remain with the self as the original object. Interestingly, Freud here suggests that narcissism might be the stage in which the 'coalescence' of drives takes place: 'This masochism would thus be evidence of and a remainder from, the phase of development in which the coalescence, which is so important for life, between the death instinct and Eros took place.'[1]

Secondary masochism is accountable via the reintrojection of aggression. Given the earlier process of projection of aggression, to the parental object, identifications and introjections, via superego formation, would reintroduce the defused aggressive impulses —now turned towards the self by the super-ego . . . and thereby produce secondary masochism.

Sadism also concerns the fusion of aggression and libido but differs with regard to the object. Sadism is a 'normal' phenomenon and the degree of pathological sadism is defined in part by the proportions of aggression that are present in the fused drive:

'Modifications in the proportions of the fusion between the instincts have the most tangible results. A surplus of sexual aggressiveness will turn a lover into a sex murderer, while a sharp diminution will make him bashful or impotent.'[2]

This formulation is somewhat out of context, as presented here, since it does not always follow that an increase in aggression must necessarily be turned against external objects. Structural contingencies are relevant as to whether or not an increase in aggression will be directed outwards, towards others, or inwards in the form of self punishment, depression, suicide.

[1] (1924c) 'The Economic Problem of Masochism, S.E., Vol. 19, p. 164.
[2] (1940a [1938]) *An Outline of Psycho-Analysis*, S.E., Vol. 23, p. 149.

Ambivalence was given passing reference by Freud in a discussion of obsessional neurosis. He wondered if 'normal ambivalence' was not a product of defusion, but he left the suggestion with the conclusion that ambivalence is 'such a fundamental phenomenon that it more probably represents an instinctual fusion that has not been completed'.[1]

[1] (1923b) *The Ego and the Id*, S.E., Vol. 19, p. 42.

REPETITION COMPULSION

Freud's formulation of this concept may be divided historically into two phases. His first elaboration of the concept came in his important paper on technique 'Remembering, Repeating and Working-Through' (1914g).

Freud's early use of the term was descriptive and one can clearly infer an operational definition in which he identified the 'compulsion to repeat' with the tendency to act out unconscious impulses-experiences that could not be remembered. He noted that the patient will repeat or act out 'everything that has already made its way from the sources of the repressed into his manifest personality —his inhibitions and unserviceable attitudes and his pathological character traits'.[1] While such repetitions make for difficulties in the analysis, they are inescapable since they in fact constitute the only manner in which the patient can remember. This fact is hardly to be deplored since it actually provides the analyst with a transference picture of the patient's conflicts, e.g. 'the transference is itself only a piece of repetition, and that . . . repetition is a transference of the forgotten past not only on to the doctor but also on to all other aspects of the current situation'.[2] Such repetitions are not confined to either analytic treatment or the treatment room. As analysis progresses and resistance develops acting out may increase outside of treatment, a circumstance well understood as being potentially damaging to the patient and the reason for the patient's commitment not to make basic changes in his life during the course of treatment. Here Freud referred to the unavoidable 'deterioration during treatment'.

Freud returned to this subject in his paper *Beyond the Pleasure Principle* (1920g). Before taking up Freud's more complex and controversial formulations, we should note the structural and dynamic view Freud offered of this phenomenon.

The compulsion to repeat, Freud suggested, could be better understood by clarifying the character of 'resistance' to remem-

---

[1] (1914g) 'Remembering, Repeating and Working-Through', S.E., Vol. 12, p. 151.
[2] ibid., p. 151.

bering. The repressed unconscious is not responsible for such resistance since the repressed constantly strives towards discharge in action. Rather, the resistance to remembering stems from the 'coherent ego'. Somewhat later in *Inhibitions, Symptom and Anxiety* (1926d), Freud comments:

'The repressed is now, as it were, an outlaw; it is excluded from the great organization of the ego and is subject only to the laws which govern the realm of the unconscious. If, now, the danger-situation changes so that the ego has no reason for fending off a new instinctual impulse analogous to the repressed one, the consequence of the restriction of the ego which has taken place will become manifest. The new impulse will run its course under an automatic influence—or, as I should prefer to say, under the influence of the compulsion to repeat. It will follow the same path as the earlier, repressed impulse, as though the danger-situation that had been overcome still existed. The fixating factor in repression, then, is the unconscious id's compulsion to repeat—a compulsion which in normal circumstances is only done away with by the freely mobile function of the ego.'[1]

One may infer the structural relationship of super-ego-to-ego in the dynamics which determine continued repression-anticathexes. But Freud apparently did not elaborate further.

The repetition compulsion, as a descriptive and clinical concept does not seem to have been disputed. But Freud's re-formulation of the concept in *Beyond the Pleasure Principle* is interrelated to his much discussed and more philosophic hypotheses concerning the 'death instinct'.

One can briefly summarize the clinical and theoretical problems that led Freud to reconceptualize the 'repetition compulsion', *viz*: (1) Some activities of children were continuously repetitive and apparently without pleasure now or in times past, (2) anxiety dreams could not be fully explained by the rule that all dreams are attempts at wish fulfilments, (3) traumatic neuroses perpetuate traumatic experiences that are not pleasurable, and (4) analytic patients continuously illustrate that they preserve and perpetually repeat experiences some of which could never have been pleasurable. By 1920, Freud appears to have condensed the 'pleasure-

[1] (1926d) *Inhibitions, Symptom and Anxiety*, S.E., Vol. 20, p. 153.

pain principle' to the 'pleasure principle'. Freud saw, in the examples given, what appeared to him exceptions to the 'pleasure principle' something beyond or prior to the pleasure principle itself, something of an instinctual quality:

'But how is the predicate of being "instinctual" (*triebhaft*) related to the compulsion to repeat? At this point we cannot escape a suspicion that we may have come upon the track of a universal attribute of instincts and perhaps of organic life in general which has not hitherto been clearly recognized or at least not explicitly stressed (last six words added 1921). *It seems, then, that an instinct is an urge inherent in organic life to restore an earlier state of things* which the living entity has been obliged to abandon under the pressure of external disturbing forces; that is, it is a kind of organic elasticity, or, to put it another way, the expression of the inertia inherent in organic life.'[1]

In summary, one may define 'the repetition compulsion' as an organic, instinctual tendency which outweighs and precedes the pleasure principle. In effect, the pleasure principle is considered as a 'tendency operating in the service of a function (the repetition compulsion) whose business it is to free the mental apparatus from excitation or to keep the amount of excitation in it constant or to keep it as low as possible'.[2]

[1] (1920g) *Beyond the Pleasure Principle*, S.E., Vol. 18, p. 36.
[2] ibid., p. 62.

ACTIVITY-PASSIVITY;
MASCULINITY-FEMININITY

See Concepts: Bisexuality and Oedipus Complex

Definition

'Activity and passivity' and 'masculinity and femininity' are two aspects of psychological sexuality. Using these terms as they have been gradually developed and defined by Freud, it can be said that 'activity and passivity' is a polarity which relates to the aims of instincts, while 'masculinity and femininity' is a more complex polarity which primarily relates to the choice of the post-oedipal sexual object and the corresponding predominance of active or passive wishes towards that object.

Freud shows that in the pre-oedipal stages of development both boys and girls have active and passive instinctual aims, and in these stages the nature of the attachment to objects and the variations in object relationships depend more on the child's phase of development and instinctual aims than on whether the child is a boy or a girl.

Both boys and girls, therefore, have active and passive, oral, anal and phallic wishes, but during the phallic phase the sex of the child begins to play a more decisive part; the boy becomes aware that females have no penis, i.e. are 'castrated', and the girl becomes aware that her erotogenic organ, the clitoris, is inferior to and no real substitute for the penis.

In the oedipal phase and its resolution, these anatomical facts play a significant part in differentiating the psychological development of boys from girls. The oedipus complex offers the boy two main possibilities of satisfaction, an active wish towards the mother which would involve usurping the father's place, or a passive wish towards the father involving taking the mother's place. As the gratification of either wish invokes the threat of castration, the boy's narcissistic cathexis of his penis impels his ego to turn away from both parents and from the oedipus complex.

The girl's development is different: in the oedipal phase her lack of a penis induces her to repress her active phallic wishes and to substitute the wish for a child in place of the wish for a penis; with

95

this purpose in view, she turns away from her mother who becomes an object of jealousy, and takes instead her father as a love-object. There is not, therefore, in girls the same decisive turning away from the oedipus complex as a whole as there is in boys.

In puberty the sexual polarity coincides with masculinity and femininity. Masculinity combines the factors of subject, activity, and possession of the penis, and the boy's development therefore continues in line with his earlier phallic development. Femininity combines the factors of object and passivity; here the girl's development is not in line with her earlier phallic development, and Freud suggests that the first phase of puberty in the girl necessitates a new measure of repression against her earlier clitoridal (phallic) sexuality in order that the vagina may become her main sexual zone and subserve the passive wish to be given a child which thus establishes her feminine sexuality.

There are numerous cases of adults, however, where there is a divergence from the normal development in respect to the sexual object and the predominant sexual aim, i.e. there is not the full masculine or feminine correspondence. To show the nature of both these factors it is necessary to differentiate between

(a) active-homosexual	
(b) passive-homosexual	instinctual
(c) active-heterosexual	aim and
(d) passive-heterosexual	object-choice

Historical Development

In the *Three Essays on the Theory of Sexuality* (1905), Freud refers to the fact that 'certain among the impulses to perversion occur regularly as pairs of opposites; and this . . . has a high theoretical significance. It is, moreover, a suggestive fact that the existence of the pair of opposites formed by sadism and masochism cannot be attributed merely to the element of aggressiveness. We should rather be inclined to connect the simultaneous presence of these opposites with the opposing masculinity and femininity which are combined in bisexuality'. A development in Freud's thinking is shown by the fact that a clause was added in the 1915 edition, saying: '. . . A contrast whose significance is reduced in psycho-analysis to that between activity and passivity'. In 1924, the wording of this added clause was slightly modified; not, however, its content.[1]

[1] (1905d) *Three Essays on the Theory of Sexuality*, S.E., Vol. 7, p. 160 and n. 2.

These changes show that Freud increasingly saw the contrast between masculinity and femininity in terms of activity versus passivity. In this sense, the psycho-analytic distinction between masculinity and femininity as a developmental process is in contrast to the layman's assessment of a difference either based on the physical sexual characteristics which are usually present and apparent at birth, or of a difference based on environmental social factors. Freud makes it quite explicit that physical sexual characteristics do not parallel mental characteristics or sexual attitudes and behaviour.[1]

Later in the same paper Freud states that the antithesis active-passive developmentally precedes that of masculine-feminine: 'A second pre-genital phase is that of the sadistic-anal organization. Here the opposition between two currents, which runs through all sexual life, is already developed; they cannot yet, however, be described as "masculine" and "feminine" but only as "active" and "passive". The *activity* is put into operation by the instinct for mastery through the agency of the somatic musculature; the organ which, more than any other, represents the *passive* sexual aim is the erotogenic mucous membrane of the anus. Both of these currents have objects, which, however, are not identical. Alongside these, other component instincts operate in an auto-erotic manner. In this phase, therefore, sexual polarity and an extraneous object are already observable. But organization and subordination to the reproductive function are still absent.'[2]

Although the case-history of Dora was also published in 1905, it was written in 1901 and already refers to the problem of bi-sexuality: 'Her declaration that she had been able to keep abreast with her brother up to the time of her first illness, but that after that she had fallen behind him in her studies, was in a certain sense also a "screen memory". It was as though she had been a boy up till that moment, and had then become girlish for the first time. She had in truth been a wild creature; but after the "asthma" she became quiet and well-behaved. That illness formed the boundary between two phases of her sexual life, of which the first was masculine in character, and the second feminine.'[3]

In the *Three Essays* Freud also examines the question of sexual

[1] ibid., p. 141 f. [2] ibid., p. 198.
[3] (1905e [1901]) 'Fragment of an Analysis of a Case of Hysteria', S.E., Vol. 7, p. 82 n. 1.

THE THEORY OF INSTINCTS

development and bisexuality in detail, and states that at the stage of the primacy of the genital zone, 'the new sexual aim assigns very different functions to the two sexes, [so] their sexual development now diverges greatly. That of males is the more straightforward and the more understandable, while that of females actually enters upon a kind of involution'.[1] 'As we all know, it is not until puberty that the sharp distinction is established between the masculine and feminine characters. . . . The auto-erotic activity of the eroto-genic zones . . . [has been] the same in both sexes, and owing to this uniformity there is no possibility of a distinction between the two sexes such as arises after puberty. So far as the auto-erotic and masturbatory manifestations of sexuality are concerned, we might lay it down that the sexuality of little girls is of a wholly masculine character'.[2]

Freud states that the clitoris is the leading erotogenic zone of little girls at the time when their sexual development still parallels that of boys; and that later, in puberty, while there is a great accession of libido in boys, there is in girls a fresh wave of repression directed towards their clitoridal, masculine sexuality. Ideally, when the girl reaches full maturity, the last function of the clitoris should be to transmit the sexual excitation to the vagina, which should then remain the main erotogenic zone in sexual intercourse. A man, however, retains his leading erotogenic zone [the penis] unchanged from childhood, nor is there a wave of repression at puberty directed towards his masculine sexuality.[3]

Clinical material, illustrating the vicissitudes of male and female sexual development, is given in 'The Taboo of Virginity' (1918) where Freud shows that the girl's childhood 'envy for the penis' is associated with strong hostile feelings towards the more fortunate boys, and that it is only later that the wish for a penis becomes the wish for a child, and that the earlier masculine constellation may be reactivated by the first act of intercourse;[4] and in the Schreber Case (1911) Freud refers to the man's feminine wish to be a woman submitting to intercourse.[5]

In 1913 Freud returns to the question of the confusion of the terms 'masculine' and 'feminine' with the qualities of 'activity'

[1] (1905d) *Three Essays on the Theory of Sexuality*, S.E., Vol. 7, p. 207.
[2] ibid., p. 219.   [3] ibid., p. 220.
[4] (1918a) 'The Taboo of Virginity', S.E., Vol. 11, p. 204.
[5] (1911c) 'Psycho-Analytic Notes on an Autobiographical Account of a Case of Paranoia (Dementia Paranoides)', S.E., Vol. 12, p. 42.

and 'passivity' and says that these latter qualities are determined not by the instincts themselves but by their aims. 'Infantile sexuality exhibits two other characteristics which are of importance from a biological point of view. It turns out to be put together from a number of component instincts which seem to be attached to certain regions of the body ("erotogenic zones") and some of which emerge from the beginning in pairs of opposites—instincts with an active and a passive aim.[1]

'In spite of all our efforts to prevent biological terminology and considerations from dominating psychoanalytic work, we cannot avoid using them even in our descriptions of the phenomena that we study. We cannot help regarding the term "instinct" as a concept on the frontier between the spheres of psychology and biology. We speak, too, of "masculine" and "feminine" mental attributes and impulses, although, strictly speaking, the differences between the sexes can lay claim to no special psychical characterization. What we speak of in ordinary life as "masculine" or "feminine" reduces itself from the point of view of psychology to the qualities of "activity" and "passivity"—that is, to qualities determined not by the instincts themselves but by their aims. The regular association of these "active" and "passive" instincts in mental life reflects the bisexuality of individuals, which is among the clinical postulates of psychoanalysis.'[2]

In 1915, in 'Instincts and their Vicissitudes', Freud considers the question of instincts with active and passive aims in detail. He comments that 'Every instinct is a piece of activity; if we speak loosely of passive instincts, we can only mean instincts whose *aim* is passive.'[3] He also states that 'Reversal of an instinct into its opposite resolves on closer examination into two different processes; a change from activity to passivity, and a reversal of its content. . . .'

Examples of the first process are met with in the two pairs of opposites: sadism–masochism and scopophilia–exhibitionism. The reversal affects only the *aims* of the instincts. The active aim (to torture, to look at) is replaced by the passive aim (to be tortured, to be looked at). Reversal of *content* is found in the single instance of

---

[1] (1913j) 'The Claims of Psycho-Analysis to Scientific Interest', S.E., Vol. 13, p. 181.
[2] ibid., p. 182.
[3] (1915c) 'Instincts and their Vicissitudes', S.E., Vol. 14, pp. 122 and 127.

the transformation of love into hate.'[1] Freud comments that both aspects may be satisfied simultaneously, e.g. masochism is actually sadism turned round upon the subject's own body, and he continues: 'The essence of the process is thus the change of the *object*, while the aim remains unchanged. We cannot fail to notice, however, that in these examples the turning round upon the subject's self and the transformation from activity to passivity converge or coincide.'[2] In other words: the active aim is to torture, then to torture oneself instead of the object, hence to be tortured—the instinct now has a passive aim. At this point Freud doubted the existence of a primary masochism; a view which he reversed later in 'The Economic Problem of Masochism' (1924); see also concept: masochism.

Freud states that with regard to sadism and scopophilia 'it should be remarked that their transformation by a reversal from activity to passivity and by a turning round upon the subject never in fact involves the whole quota of the instinctural impulse. The earlier active direction of the instinct persists to some degree side by side with its later passive direction.[3] (It is interesting that Freud here described this co-existence as "ambivalence".)'[4]

He also comments that the first stage is one where the person's own body is the object of the scopophilic instinct, and must therefore be classed under narcissism; that the active aim is directed towards someone else's body and hence involves object-cathexis, while the passive aim holds fast to the narcissistic object—the person's own body. Thus the term 'passive scopophilic instinct' seems to refer only to the first developmental phase of auto-erotism where the scopophilic instinct finds satisfaction on the subject's own body. 'We have become accustomed to call the early phase of the development of the ego, during which its sexual instincts find auto-erotic satisfaction, "narcissism", without at once entering on any discussion of the relation between auto-erotism and narcissism. It follows that the preliminary stage of the scopophilic instinct, in which the subject's own body is the object of the scopophilia, must be classed under narcissism, and that we must describe it as a narcissistic formation. The active scopophilic instinct develops from this, by leaving narcissism behind. The passive scopophilic instinct, on the contrary, holds fast to the narcissistic object.

---

[1] (1915c) 'Instincts and their Vicissitudes', S.E., Vol. 14, p. 127.
[2] ibid., p. 127.   [3] ibid., p. 130.   [4] ibid., p. 131 and n2.

Similarly, the transformation of sadism into masochism implies a return to the narcissistic object. And in both these cases [i.e. in passive scopophilia and masochism] the narcissistic *subject* is, through identification, replaced by another, extraneous ego. If we take into account our constructed preliminary narcissistic stage of sadism, we shall be approaching a more general realization—namely, that the instinctual vicissitudes which consist in the instinct's being turned round upon the subject's own ego and under-going reversal from activity to passivity are dependent on the narcissistic organization of the ego and bear the stamp of that phase. They perhaps correspond to the attempts at defence which at higher stages of the development of the ego are effected by other means.'[1]

Freud said that he had only discussed the vicissitudes of sadism and scopophilia because insufficient was known about the other 'ambivalent' sexual instincts, but he further suggests that these first two instincts have a special significance in that they have great need for an object in order to attain satisfaction, whereas other instincts may be auto-erotic, i.e. 'their object is negligible in comparison with the *organ* which is their source, and as a rule coincides with that organ'. Freud quotes 'a plausible suggestion of Federn (1913) and Jekels (1913)', that, 'the form and function of the organ determine the activity or passivity of the instinctual aim'.[2]

In connection with the antithesis 'loving–being loved', Freud says this 'corresponds exactly to the transformation from activity to passivity and may be traced to an underlying situation in the same way as . . . the scopophilic instinct. This situation is that of *loving oneself*, which we regard as the characteristic feature of narcissism. Then, according as the object or the subject is replaced by an extraneous one, what results is the active aim of loving or the passive one of being loved—the latter remaining near to narcis-sism'.[3] 'The antithesis active–passive must not be confused with the antithesis ego-subject—external world-object. The relation of the ego to the external world is passive so far as it receives stimuli from it but active when it reacts to these . . . the ego-subject is passive in respect to external stimuli but active through its own instincts. The antithesis active-passive coalesces later with the antithesis masculine-feminine, which, until this has taken place, has no psychological meaning. The coupling of activity with

[1] ibid., p. 131 f.   [2] ibid., p. 132 f.   [3] ibid., p. 133.

masculinity and of passivity with femininity meets us, indeed, as a biological fact; but it is by no means so invariably complete and exclusive as we are inclined to assume.'[1] (Freud discusses this point at greater length in a footnote which he added to the *Three Essays* in 1915.)[2]

Freud concludes this section: 'We may sum up by saying that the essential feature in the vicissitudes undergone by instincts lies in *the subjection of the instinctual impulses to the influences of three great polarities that dominate mental life.* Of these three polarities we might describe that of activity–passivity as the *biological*, that of ego-external world as the *real*, and finally that of pleasure–unpleasure as the *economic* polarity.'[3]

Slightly earlier (1914), when criticizing Adler's concept of 'The Masculine Protest', Freud comments that, 'Children have, to begin with, no idea of the significance of the distinction between the sexes'; they start with the assumption that the penis is possessed by both sexes.[4]

In the paper 'On Narcissism' (1914) there is a detailed exposition of the development of object-choice. This starts from the point when the child has two sexual objects—himself and his mother. Later he may make either a narcissistic or an anaclictic object-choice. 'Complete object-love of the attachment type is, properly speaking, characteristic of the male. It displays the marked sexual overvaluation which is doubtless derived from the child's original narcissism and thus corresponds to a transference of that narcissism to the sexual object. . . . A different course is followed in the type of female most frequently met with . . . [puberty] seems to bring about an intensification of the original narcissism, and this is unfavourable to the development of a true object-choice with its accompanying sexual overvaluation. . . . Nor does their [women's] need lie in the direction of loving, but of being loved.'[5] However, 'In the child which they bear, a part of their own body confronts them like an extraneous object, to which, starting out from their narcissism, they can then give complete object-love. There are other

---

[1] (1915c) 'Instincts and their Vicissitudes, S.E., Vol. 14, p. 134.
[2] (1905d [1915]) *Three Essays on The Theory of Sexuality*, S.E., Vol. 7, p. 219 n1.
[3] (1915c) 'Instincts and their Vicissitudes', S.E., Vol. 14, p. 140.
[4] (1914d) 'On the History of the Psycho-Analytic Movement', S.E., Vol. 14, p. 55.
[5] (1914c) 'On Narcissism: An Introduction', S.E., Vol. 14, p. 88 f.

women, again, who do not have to wait for a child in order to take the step in development from (secondary) narcissism to object-love. Before puberty they feel masculine and develop some way along masculine lines; after this trend has been cut short on their reaching female maturity, they still retain the capacity of longing for a masculine ideal.'[1]

In 1916–17, Freud wrote a series of *Introductory Lectures on Psycho-Analysis*, in one of which he summarized the early phases of sexual organization. Referring to the pre-genital organization, when the sadistic and anal instincts are most prominent he states: 'The contrast between "masculine" and "feminine" plays no part here as yet. Its place is taken by the contrast between "active" and "passive". . . . What appears to us as masculine in the activities of this phase, when we look at it from the point of view of the genital phase, turns out to be the expression of an instinct for mastery which easily passes over into cruelty. Trends with a passive aim are attached to the erotogenic zone of the anal orifice. . . . The instincts for looking and for gaining knowledge [the scopophilic and epistemophilic instincts] are powerfully at work. . . . The component instincts of this phase are not without objects, but those objects do not necessarily converge into a single object.'[2]

Further clinical material is given in the case history of the Wolf-man, which shows the contrast between an early childhood stage of active sadistic fantasies and behaviour and the later adult passive, masochistic fantasies, this is linked with a contrast between the boy's first making a female object choice, and, after being rejected by her, seeking another sexual object, i.e. his father, but with a passive aim. The effect of external events which forced him into a passive role (e.g. seduction by his elder sister, observation of parental intercourse) is also traced.[3] This case history also contains a summary of the patient's psychopathology linking the early wavering between activity and passivity with the adolescent struggle for masculinity, and shows that the narcissistic component was decisive in forming and maintaining his homosexual attitude.[4]

In another paper, Freud traces the vicissitudes of the woman's repressed wish to possess a penis. He shows that it may form

[1] ibid., p. 89 f.

[2] (1916–17) *Introductory Lectures on Psycho-Analysis*, S.E., Vol. 16, p. 327.

[3] (1918b [1914]) 'From the History of an Infantile Neurosis', S.E., Vol. 17, pp. 26 f., 109 (cf. also ibid., pp. 64, 79, 84, 101 f., 110–12 and 117 n.).

[4] ibid., p. 118.

neurotic symptoms, or it may have been transformed into the wish for a baby, or into the wish for a man—which by determining the object-choice enables a part of narcissistic masculinity to serve the female sexual function, i.e. to be changed into femininity.[1]

In a further paper, the differences and similarities between sadistic and masochistic fantasies in girls and boys are discussed: 'It must not be forgotten that when a boy's incestuous fantasy is transformed into the corresponding masochistic one, one more reversal has to take place than in the case of a girl, namely the substitution of passivity for activity; and this additional degree of distortion may save the fantasy from having to remain unconscious as a result of repression. In this way the sense of guilt would be satisfied by regression instead of by repression. In the female cases the sense of guilt, in itself perhaps more exacting, could be appeased only by a combination of the two.'[2] In the same paper Freud states: 'We are justified in assuming that no great change is effected by the *repression* of the original unconscious fantasy. Whatever is repressed from consciousness or replaced in it by something else remains intact and potentially operative in the unconscious. The effect of *regression* to an earlier stage of the sexual organization is quite another matter . . . the state of things changes in the unconscious as well. Thus in both sexes the masochistic fantasy of being beaten by the father, though not the passive fantasy of being loved by him, lives on in the unconscious after repression has taken place.'[3]

In 'A Case of Female Homosexuality' (1920) Freud differentiated between the questions of object-choice on the one hand and of the sexual characteristics and sexual attitudes of the subject on the other:

'A man with predominantly male [social] characteristics and also masculine in his erotic life [instinctual aims] may still be inverted in respect to his object, loving only men instead of women. A man in whose character feminine attributes obviously predominate, who may, indeed, behave in love like a woman, might be expected, from this feminine attitude, to choose a man for his love-object; but he may nevertheless be heterosexual, and show no more inversion in respect to his object than an average normal man. The

[1] (1917c) 'On Transformations of Instincts as Exemplified in Anal Erotism', S.E., Vol. 17, p. 129.
[2] (1919e) 'A Child is Being Beaten', S.E., Vol. 17, p. 190.
[3] ibid., p. 199.

same is true of women; here also mental sexual character and object-choice do not necessarily coincide. . . . [Homosexuality] is instead a question of three sets of characteristics, namely:

Physical sexual characters (physical hermaphroditism)
Mental sexual characters (masculine or feminine attitude)
Kind of object-choice.'[1]

In his paper on the infantile genital organization (1923), Freud elaborated and gave a very clear summary of his views on sexual polarity. 'A first antithesis is introduced with the choice of object, which, of course, presupposes a subject and an object. At the stage of the pregenital sadistic-anal organization, there is as yet no question of male and female; the antithesis between *active* and *passive* is the dominant one. At the following stage of infantile genital organization . . . *maleness* exists, but not femaleness. The antithesis here is between having a *male genital* and being *castrated*. It is not until development has reached its completion at puberty that the sexual polarity coincides with *male* and *female*. Maleness combines [the factors of] subject, activity and possession of the penis; femaleness takes over [those of] object and passivity. The vagina is now valued as a place of shelter for the penis; it enters into the heritage of the womb.'[2]

In 'The Dissolution of the Oedipus Complex' (1924), Freud shows that the oedipus complex offers the child 'two possibilities of satisfaction, an active and a passive one'. The boy can put himself either in father's or mother's place; both involve castration—either as a punishment, or as a feminine identification. Therefore the boy allies with his narcissistic interest in his penis against the libidinal cathexis of his parental objects—the boy's ego turns away from the oedipus complex.[3]

In another paper, Freud states that the boy's wanting to take his mother's place as the love object of his father, in the oedipal situation, is described as the feminine attitude.[4] Discussing female development in the same paper, Freud comments

[1] (1920a) 'The Psychogenesis of a Case of Female Homosexuality', S.E., Vol. 18, p. 170.
[2] (1923e) 'The Infantile Genital Organization of the Libido', S.E., Vol. 19, p. 145.
[3] (1924d) 'The Dissolution of the Oedipus Complex', S.E., Vol. 19, p. 176.
[4] (1925j) 'Some Psychological Consequences of the Anatomical Distinction between the Sexes', S.E., Vol. 19, p. 250.

that in the phallic phase, soon after the appearance of penis-envy, the girl develops strong impulses *against* masturbation. He considers these impulses to be due to a narcissistic sense of humiliation (the clitoris being so inferior to the penis), and that they form a fore-runner to the wave of repression at puberty, which removes a large part of the girl's masculine sexuality.[1] In discussing the girl's oedipal situation, Freud says: 'She gives up her wish for a penis and puts in place of it a wish for a child: and *with that purpose in view* she takes her father as a love-object. Her mother becomes the object of her jealousy. . . . When the girl's attachment to her father comes to grief later on . . . it may give place to an identification with him and the girl may thus return to her masculinity complex and perhaps remain fixated in it.' Freud then comments on the paradox that the castration complex destroys the oedipus complex in boys, but in girls it makes possible and leads up to the oedipus complex, and says, 'This contradiction is cleared up if we reflect that the castration complex always operates in the sense implied in its subject-matter: it inhibits and limits masculinity and encourages femininity.' The difference between male and female sexual development at this stage corresponds to the difference between a castration that has been carried out and one that has merely been threatened.[2] Freud then goes on to discuss the differences in super-ego formation in girls and boys; this is linked with the full shattering of the oedipus complex in boys but does not happen to the same extent in girls.

In *Inhibitions, Symptoms and Anxiety* (1926) Freud gives clinical material illustrating the factors underlying a passive sexual attitude; he compares two cases (Little Hans and the Wolf Man) to show the differences in degree of the underlying instinctual regression and the differences in the nature of the instinctual wishes defended against in the phobic symptoms.[3]

In *Civilization and its Discontents* (1930), Freud re-states his views on bisexuality; 'We are accustomed to say that every human being displays both male and female instinctual impulses, needs and attributes', and after pointing out that we should not too readily equate activity with maleness and passivity with femaleness, he

---

[1] (1925j) 'Some Psychological Consequences of the Anatomical Distinction between the Sexes', S.E., Vol. 19. pp. 255–56.

[2] ibid., p. 256 f.

[3] (1926d) *Inhibitions, Symptoms and Anxiety*, S.E., Vol. 20, pp. 105–8, and 124.

says: 'If we assume it as a fact that each individual seeks to satisfy both male and female wishes in his sexual life, we are prepared for the possibility that those [two sets of] demands are not fulfilled by the same object, and that they interfere with each other unless they can be kept apart and each impulse guided into a particular channel that is suited to it. Another difficulty arises from the circumstance that there is so often associated with the erotic relationship, over and above its own sadistic components, a quota of plain inclination to aggression.'[1]

In 'Female Sexuality' (1931), there is a long discussion of the *active* element in the little girl's attitude towards her mother and in femininity in general. Freud mentions the child's early tendency to repeat actively that which it has experienced passively, whether the experience was pleasant or unpleasant. He mentions that the extent of this swingover from passivity to activity varies a great deal from child to child, and says that a child's behaviour in this respect may enable us to draw conclusions as to the relative strength of the masculinity and femininity that it will exhibit in its sexuality. He points out that what finds expression in a girl's playing with dolls is not true femininity but an active repetition of a passive experience.[2] The transformations of the little girl's aggressive oral and sadistic wishes are mentioned, and the emergence of the little girl's wish to impregnate her mother. Freud also outlines the three paths which diverge from the point when the little girl discovers her organic inferiority of clitoris versus penis— (a) the one which leads to a cessation of her whole sexual life, (b) the one which leads to a defiant over-emphasis of her masculinity, and (c) the first steps towards definitive femininity.[3]

In 'Dostoevsky and Parricide' (1928), Freud had amplified his views on the boy's development, particularly in regard to the aggressive component. He showed that a boy's relation to his father is an ambivalent one, and that the trends of hate and tenderness both combine to produce a masculine identification with the father.[4] He also refers to super-ego formation: 'If the father was hard, violent and cruel, the super-ego takes over those attributes from him and, in the relations between the ego and it, the passivity

[1] (1930a) *Civilization and its Discontents*, S.E., Vol. 21, p. 106 n.
[2] (1931b) 'Female Sexuality', S.E., Vol. 21, p. 236 f.
[3] ibid., pp. 232 and 237–9.
[4] (1928b) 'Dostoevsky and Parricide', S.E., Vol. 21, p. 183 f.

which was supposed to have been repressed is re-established. The super-ego has become sadistic, and the ego becomes masochistic—that is to say, at bottom passive in a feminine way.'[1]

In the *New Introductory Lectures on Psycho-Analysis* (1933) Freud recapitulates but also comprehensively draws together all the aspects of female sexuality which had hitherto been mentioned separately in his earlier papers.[2] Freud comments on the fact that where the woman's object-choice does not meet with any serious internal or external obstacles, it is often made according to the narcissistic ideal of the man whom the girl would have liked to be.[3] He also refers to the two levels underlying the girl's identification with her mother—the 'affectionate' pre-oedipal attachment and the oedipal hostility, he adds that the phase of the tender pre-oedipal attachment is the decisive one for her acquisitions of those characteristics which are necessary for her later femininity to be successful.[4]

In 'Analysis Terminable and Interminable' (1937), Freud mentions two prominent analytic themes (the wish for a penis in women, and the struggle against passivity in men) which are very troublesome to analyse.

'The two corresponding themes are in the female, an *envy for the penis*—a positive striving to possess a male genital—and, in the male a struggle against his passive or feminine attitude to another male. What is common to the two themes was singled out at an early date by psychoanalytic nomenclature as an attitude towards the castration complex. Subsequently Alfred Adler brought the term masculine protest into current use. It fits the case of males perfectly; but I think that, from the start, repudiation of femininity would have been the correct description of this remarkable feature in the psychical life of human beings.

'This factor . . . cannot, by its very nature, occupy the same position in both sexes. In males the striving to be masculine is completely ego-syntonic from the first; the passive attitude, since it presupposes an acceptance of castration, is energetically repressed, and often its presence is only indicated by excessive

---

[1] (1928b) 'Dostoevsky and Parricide', S.E., Vol. 21, p. 185.
[2] (1933a) *New Introductory Lectures on Psycho-Analysis*, S.E., Vol. 22, pp. 114–16, 117 n, 120, 126, 128–31.
[3] ibid., p. 132.   [4] ibid., p. 134.

over-compensations. In females, too, the striving to be masculine is ego-syntonic at a certain period—namely in the phallic phase, before the development to femininity has set in. But it then succumbs to the momentous process of repression whose outcome . . . determines the fortunes of a woman's femininity. A great deal depends on whether a sufficient amount of her masculinity complex escapes repression and exercises a permanent influence on her character. Normally, large portions of the complex are transformed and contribute to the construction of her femininity: the appeased wish for a penis is destined to be converted into a wish for a baby and for a husband, who possesses a penis. It is strange, however, how often we find that the wish for masculinity has been retained in the unconscious and, from out of its state of repression, exercises a disturbing influence.

'As will be seen from what I have said, in both cases it is the attitude proper to the opposite sex which has succumbed to repression.'[1]

At the end of this section, Freud adds a footnote emphasizing what he did *not* mean by the terms active–passive:

'We must not be misled by the term "masculine protest" into supposing that what the man is repudiating is his passive attitude (as such)—what might be called the social aspect of femininity. Such a view is contradicted by an observation that is easily verifiable—namely that such men often display a masochistic attitude—a state that amounts to bondage—towards women. What they reject is not passivity in general, but passivity towards a male. In other words, the "masculine protest" is in fact nothing else than castration anxiety.'[2]

Finally, in *An Outline of Psycho-Analysis* (1938), Freud says, when discussing the effects of the castration complex in boys and girls:

'The results of the threat of castration are multifarious and incalculable; they affect the whole of a boy's relations with his father and mother and subsequently with men and women in general. As a rule the child's masculinity is unable to stand up to this first

[1] (1937c) 'Analysis Terminable and Interminable', S.E., Vol. 23, p. 250 n.
[2] ibid., p. 252 n.

shock. In order to preserve his sexual organ he renounces the possession of his mother more or less completely; his sexual life often remains permanently encumbered by the prohibition. If a strong feminine component, as we call it, is present in him, its strength is increased by this intimidation of his masculinity. He falls into a passive attitude to his father, such as he attributes to his mother. It is true that as a result of the threat he has given up masturbation, but not the activities of his imagination accompanying it. On the contrary, since these are now the only form of sexual satisfaction remaining to him, he indulges in them more than before and in these fantasies, though he still continues to identify himself with his father, he also does so, simultaneously and perhaps predominantly, with his mother. Derivatives and modified products of these early masturbatory fantasies usually make their way into his later ego and play a part in the formation of his character. Apart from this encouragement of his femininity, fear and hatred of his father gain greatly in intensity. The boy's masculinity withdraws, as it were, into a defiant attitude towards his father, which will dominate his later behaviour in human society in a compulsive fashion. A residue of his erotic fixation to his mother is often left in the form of an excessive dependence on her, and this persists as a kind of bondage to women. He no longer ventures to love his mother, but he cannot risk not being loved by her, for in that case he would be in danger of being betrayed by her to his father and handed over to castration.'[1]

A few pages later Freud continues:

'The effects of the castration complex in little girls are more uniform and no less profound. A female child has, of course, no need to fear the loss of a penis; she must, however, react to the fact of not having received one. . . . If during the phallic phase she tries to get pleasure like a boy by the manual stimulation of her genitals, it often happens that she fails to obtain sufficient satisfaction and extends her judgement of inferiority from her stunted penis to her whole self. . . .

'If a little girl persists in her first wish—to grow into a boy—in extreme cases she will end as a manifest homosexual, and otherwise she will exhibit markedly masculine traits in the conduct of

[1] (1940a [1938]) *An Outline of Psycho-Analysis*, S.E., Vol. 23, p. 190 f.

her later life, will choose a masculine vocation, and so on. The other path leads by way of abandoning the mother she has loved: the daughter, under the influence of her envy for the penis, cannot forgive her mother for having sent her into the world so insufficiently equipped. In her resentment over this she gives up her mother and puts someone else in her place as the object of her love—her father. If one has lost a love-object, the most obvious reaction is to identify oneself with it, to replace it from within, as it were, by identification. This mechanism now comes to the little girl's help. Identification with her mother can take the place of attachment to her mother . . . she tries to take her mother's place with her father, and begins to hate the mother she used to love, and from two motives: from jealousy as well as from mortification over the penis she has been denied. Her new relation to her father may start by having as its content a wish to have his penis at her disposal, but it culminates in another wish—to have a baby from him as a gift. . . .

'It does little harm to a woman if she remains in her feminine oedipus attitude. (The term "electra complex" has been proposed for it.) She will in that case choose her husband for his paternal characteristics and be ready to recognize his authority. Her longing to possess a penis, which is in fact unappeasable, may find satisfaction if she can succeed in completing her love for the organ by extending it to the bearer of the organ, just as happened earlier when she progressed from her mother's breast to her mother as a whole person.'[1]

[1] ibid., p. 193 f.

MASOCHISM

'Masochism' is the term to describe the fusion between destructiveness directed inwards and sexuality,[1] a certain amount of which is always present in normal sexual relations, though in extreme cases of perversion it causes the subject to suffer pain, ill treatment and humiliation as the main or even sole sexual aim.[2] Freud discussed it for the first time in his *Three Essays on the Theory of Sexuality* (1905d) but his final formulations only appeared twenty years later in 'The Economic Problem of Masochism' (1924c). Three main phases can be distinguished in the development of Freud's conceptualization of masochism:

(a) 1905–19, when he discussed masochism almost exclusively as a perversion, as a transformation of sadism, and had serious doubts as to the existence of primary masochism.

(b) 1919–24, when masochism was not only seen in the light of a perversion, but as a regressive phenomenon due to an unconscious need for punishment. In 1920 the existence of primary masochism was first mentioned as a possibility.

(c) 1924–37, when—in connection with the theory of the death instinct—Freud postulated a primary as well as a secondary masochism and further distinguished the three forms of erotogenic, feminine, and moral masochism.

(a) *1905–19*
From the earliest formulations onwards Freud recognized the close link between masochistic tendencies and the sexual instincts, speaking of the 'masochistic components of the sexual instinct'.[3] He considered the erotogenic effects of painful feelings as one of he main roots of the masochistic-sadistic instinct.[4] He went so far as to define masochism as comprising 'any passive attitude towards

[1] (1930a) *Civilization and its Discontents*, S.E., Vol. 21, p. 119 n.
[2] (1933a) *New Introductory Lectures on Psycho-Analysis*, S.E., Vol. 22, p. 135 n.
[3] (1900a) *The Interpretation of Dreams*, S.E., Vol. 4–5, p. 159; cf. also (1905d) *Three Essays on the Theory of Sexuality*, S.E., Vol. 7, p. 150 n.
[4] (1905d) *Three Essays on the Theory of Sexuality*, S.E., Vol. 7, p. 204.

sexual life and the sexual object, the extreme instance of which appears to be that in which satisfaction is conditional upon suffering physical or mental pain at the hands of the sexual object'.[1] These extreme cases are to be considered as perversions which are the result of the exaggeration and fixation of the original passive sexual aim.[2]

But even as perversions both sadism and masochism occupy a special position 'since the contrast between activity and passivity which lies behind them is among the universal characteristics of sexual life'.[3] Both the active and the passive forms of this perversion are habitually found in the same individual. Hence a sadist is always at the same time a masochist.[4] This is not only due to the element of aggressiveness but also to bisexuality.[5] The realization that there are sadistic and masochistic perverts who are capable of substituting a fantasy for real sexual satisfaction[6] marked an important step forward towards Freud's later formulations.

During this period Freud expressed his serious doubts as to whether masochism could be a primary phenomenon.[7] He rather thought that masochism always came into existence as a reversal of an aggressive, sadistic component into its opposite.[8] In 1905 he defined masochism as the 'passive instinct of cruelty',[9] and in 1915 we find the formulation that 'masochism is actually sadism turned round upon the subject's own ego', the essence of the process being the change of the object.[10] It is important to note that at this time Freud did not include self-torture and self-punishment under masochism,[11] whereas later they were considered as among the main characteristics of moral masochism. He further maintained that the reversal from activity to passivity and the turning round upon the subject involved in the transformation of sadism into masochism never 'involves the whole quota of the instinctual impulse'[12] and that the transformation 'implies a return to the

---

[1] ibid., p. 158.   [2] ibid., p. 158 f.   [3] ibid., p. 159.   [4] ibid., pp. 159, 167.
[5] ibid., p. 160.
[6] (1916–17)*Introductory Lectures on Psycho-Analysis*, S.E., Vol. 15–16, p. 257 n.
[7] (1905d) *Three Essays on the Theory of Sexuality*, S.E., Vol. 7, p. 158; cf. also (1915c) 'Instincts and their Vicissitudes', S.E., Vol. 14, p. 128.
[8] (1900a) *The Interpretation of Dreams*, S.E., Vol. 4–5, p. 159; cf. also (1905d) *Three Essays on the Theory of Sexuality*, S.E., Vol. 7, p. 158.
[9] (1905d) *Three Essays on the Theory of Sexuality*, S.E., Vol. 7, p. 193.
[10] (1915c) 'Instincts and their Vicissitudes', S.E., Vol. 14, p. 127.
[11] ibid., p. 128.   [12] ibid., p. 130.

narcissistic object'.[1] The enjoyment of pain is an aim 'which was originally masochistic, but which can only become an instinctual aim in someone who was originally sadistic'. This is probably due to the fact that the causing of pain is enjoyed masochistically by the subject through identification with the suffering object.[2]

(b) 1919–24

The paper 'A Child is Being Beaten' (1919e)— a study of beating-fantasies among boys and girls—contains many new insights into the problem of masochism. Freud himself referred to it as a paper on masochism.[3] In it he postulated that a sense of guilt is invariably the factor that transforms sadism into masochism, and that sexual love contributes an important share to its content.[4] It is this sense of guilt which, in certain patients, finds its satisfaction in the illness, and refuses to give up the punishment of suffering.[5] He characterized one form of masochism in the following way: '*It is not only the punishment for the forbidden genital relation, but also the regressive substitute for that relation*, and from this latter source it derives the libidinal excitation which is from this time forward attached to it.'[6] Although the form of such a beating-fantasy is sadistic, the satisfaction derived from it is masochistic because the libidinal cathexis of the repressed portion of the fantasy and the sense of guilt attached to that portion have been taken over.[7] In both sexes the masochistic fantasy of being beaten by the father lives on in the unconscious after repression.[8]

In 1919 Freud still held fast to the view that 'masochism is not the manifestation of a primary instinct, but originates from sadism which has been turned round upon the self—that is to say, by means of regression from an object to the ego'.[9] There is, however, already an allusion to what was later distinguished as 'feminine masochism' when Freud postulated the existence—especially among women—of instincts with a passive aim.[10]

In *Beyond the Pleasure Principle* (1920g) we find the first mention of two ideas which were fully developed in the paper on masochism four years later, namely that there are masochistic

---

[1] (1915c) 'Instincts and their Vicissitudes,' S.E., Vol. 14, p. 132.
[2] ibid., p. 129.   [3] (1919e) 'A Child is Being Beaten', S.E., Vol. 17, p. 177.
[4] ibid., p. 189.   [5] (1923b) *The Ego and the Id*, S.E., Vol. 19, p. 49 n.
[6] (1919e) 'A Child is Being Beaten', S.E., Vol. 17, p. 189.   [7] ibid., p. 190 n.
[8] ibid., p. 198 n.   [9] ibid., p. 193 n.   [10] ibid., p. 193 n.

trends of the ego[1] and that there might be such a thing as primary masochism.[2]

(c) *1924–37*

The paper on 'The Economic Problem of Masochism' (1924c) contains Freud's final formulations as regards this concept. He now differentiated two types: primary and secondary masochism; and three forms: an erotogenic masochism, out of which two later forms, feminine and moral masochism, develop.[3]

Erotogenic masochism: This is the primary masochism[4] which has a biological and constitutional basis[5] and is defined as pleasure in pain.[6] For all practical purposes it is identical with the death instinct (primal sadism) and is that portion of this instinct which has not been transposed outwards on to objects but has remained inside fused with the libido, with the self as its object. Erotogenic or primary masochism is evidence of the coalescence and fusion between the death instinct and Eros.[7] It 'accompanies the libido through all its developmental phases and derives from them its changing psychical coatings'.[8]

Feminine masochism: This is the least problematical form and the one most accessible to observation.[9] It is called feminine because the fantasies associated with it place the subject in a characteristically female situation of being castrated, copulated with, or giving birth to a baby. Many of its features also point to infantile life in that the masochist wants to be treated like a small, helpless, naughty child.[10] The condition that the suffering has to emanate from a loved person is essential.[11]

Moral masochism: This is the most important form which is determined by a mostly unconscious sense of guilt or need for punish-

---

[1] (1920g) *Beyond the Pleasure Principle*, S.E., Vol. 18, p. 13 f.

[2] ibid., p. 54 n.

[3] (1924c) 'The Economic Problem of Masochism', S.E., Vol. 19, p. 161; cf. also (1905d) *Three Essays on the Theory of Sexuality*, S.E., Vol. 7, p. 158 (added 1924).

[4] (1905d) *Three Essays on the Theory of Sexuality*, S.E., Vol. 7, p. 158 (added 1924).

[5] (1924c) 'The Economic Problem of Masochism', S.E., Vol. 19, p. 161.

[6] ibid., p. 162.　　[7] ibid., pp. 164, 170.　　[8] ibid., p. 164 n.

[9] ibid., p. 161.　　[10] ibid., p. 162.　　[11] ibid., p. 164.

ment.[1] It has loosened its connection with sexuality in that the suffering in itself is what matters, with the object being irrelevant.[2] Moral masochism has to be clearly distinguished from an unconscious extension of morality, which is characterized by the ego's submission to the heightened sadism of the super-ego, while in moral masochism it is the ego's own, largely unconscious masochism, which seeks punishment from the super-ego or authoritative external powers. In moral masochism the sadism of the super-ego and the masochism of the ego supplement each other and produce the same effect. Beating-fantasies are a regressive distortion of the wish to have passive, feminine sexual relations with the father, and constitute the hidden meaning of moral masochism, which at the same time leads to a re-sexualization of morality and to a revival of the oedipus complex.[3]

Secondary masochism: This is produced by the instinct of destruction which cannot find employment as sadism in actual life, retreats and is turned round upon the subject's own self, where part of it is superadded to the primary masochism, whereas another part is taken up by the super-ego, thus increasing its sadism.[4] This turning back of sadism against the self occurs particularly where cultural suppression of the instincts holds back a large part of the subject's destructive instinctual components from being exercised in life.[5]

Feminine and moral masochism are not to be considered as primary masochism, although Freud is not explicit about this. It is also implicit in his formulations that both can be increased by secondary masochism.

In his later works Freud clarified some further aspects in regard to masochism. He stated that masochistic impulses get reinforced by regression and can be the cause for new symptoms in obsessional neuroses.[6] Exaggerated anxiety-reactions in the face of real danger situations can be understood as a summation of realistic anxiety

[1] (1924c) 'The Economic Problem of Masochism', S.E., Vol. 19, pp. 161, 166, 169; cf. (1937c) 'Analysis Terminable and Interminable', S.E., Vol. 23, p. 242 n.
[2] ibid., p. 165.
[3] ibid., p. 169.
[4] (1905d) *Three Essays on the Theory of Sexuality*, S.E., Vol. 7, p. 158; cf. also (1924c) 'The Economic Problem of Masochism', S.E., Vol. 19, pp. 164, 170.
[5] (1924c) 'The Economic Problem of Masochism', S.E., Vol. 19, p. 170.
[6] (1926d) *Inhibitions, Symptoms and Anxiety*, S.E., Vol. 20, p. 117.

and caused by the instinct of destruction directed against the subject himself.[1] Freud also maintained that complete masochists need not necessarily be neurotic.[2] He further clarified the point that masochism is only to be called a perversion when it thrusts the other sexual aims into the background and substitutes its own aims for it. Sadism and masochism are cornerstones for the theory of aggression and destructiveness, and Freud argues that masochism is older than sadism, as the latter only comes into existence when the greater portion of the instinct of self-destruction (equated with masochism without its erotic components) is turned outwards. The destructive instinct is only observable when it is bound up with erotic instincts to form masochism or when it is turned outwards as aggressiveness.[3]

[1] ibid., p. 168 n.
[2] (1928b) 'Dostoevsky and Parricide', S.E., Vol. 21, p. 179.
[3] (1933a) *New Introductory Lectures on Psycho-Analysis*, S.E., Vol. 22, p. 135 n.

SADISM

(See Concept: Masochism)

Sadism was the term used to describe a desire to humiliate, sub-jugate and/or to inflict pain, etc., upon the sexual object, which reaches its height in the classic perversion but an element of which is present in normal sexuality.

Initially, Freud viewed sadism as one of the component instincts of the sexual instinct. He kept to this view until the formulation of a death instinct, when he considered sadism in relation to the aggressive instinct. 'But it is to be remarked that even there, and in Freud's later writings (for instance, in Chapter IV of *The Ego and the Id*), the aggressive instinct was still something secondary, derived from the primary self-destructive death instinct.'[1]

Freud's first detailed discussion of sadism is in the *Three Essays on the Theory of Sexuality*. 'As regards algolagnia, sadism, the roots are easy to detect in the normal. The sexuality of most male human beings contains an element of aggressiveness—a desire to subjugate; the biological significance of it seems to lie in the need for overcoming the resistance of the sexual object by means other than the process of wooing. Thus sadism would correspond to an aggressive component of the sexual instinct which has become independent and exaggerated and, by displacement, has usurped the leading position.'[2]

Sadism was originally thought to be the active part in the pair of component instincts sadism-masochism. It must be noted that though sadism was considered as a component of the sexual instinct, masochism was on the other hand, to start with, described by Freud not as a primary phenomenon but the result of the turning against the self of sadism. 'Sadism and masochism occupy a special position among the perversions, since the contrast be-tween activity and passivity which lies behind them is among the universal characteristics of sexual life.'[3]

[1] [Editor's Introduction] (1923b) *The Ego and the Id*, S.E., Vol. 19, p. 62.
[2] (1905d) *Three Essays on the Theory of Sexuality*, S.E., Vol. 7, p. 157 n.
[3] [1915] ibid., p. 159.

'It is, moreover, a suggestive fact that the existence of the pair of opposites formed by sadism and masochism cannot be attributed merely to the element of aggressiveness. We should rather be inclined to connect the simultaneous presence of these opposites with the opposing masculinity and femininity which are combined in bisexuality—a contrast which often has to be replaced in psychoanalysis by that between activity and passivity.[1] (The editor's footnote points out that the last clause is the 1924 version of Freud's. It is important to note this because by this time Freud had postulated the life and death instincts, and it was the time just after the structural theory was put forward in *The Ego and the Id*.)

In the analysis of melancholia, Freud shows how it is possible for one to treat oneself as an object, and in this sense turn the sadism against one's own ego, even to the point of killing oneself. 'The analysis of melancholia now shows that the ego can kill itself only if, owing to the return of the object-cathexis, it can treat itself as an object—if it is able to direct against itself the hostility which relates to an object and which represents the ego's original reaction to objects in the external world.'[2]

It was in *Beyond the Pleasure Principle* (1920g), with the formulation of life and death instincts, that Freud queried his earlier assumptions in relation to sadism and masochism, and as a component instinct of the sexual instinct. He now re-examined the question of sadism in relation to the death instinct, accepting primary masochism as a possibility. When this primary masochism is turned outside it becomes sadism. (See 'masochism' for full description.)

Freud pointed out that in sadism—as a perversion—both its active (sadism) and its passive form (masochism) always occur together, though the one or the other element of the pair may predominate. In a footnote added in 1924 to the *Three Essays*, Freud refers to his having been 'led to assign a peculiar position, based upon the origin of the instincts, to the pair of opposites constituted by sadism and masochism, and to place them outside the class of the remaining perversions.'[3]

'From the very first we recognized the presence of a sadistic

[1] [1924] ibid., p. 160.
[2] (1917e [1915]) 'Mourning and Melancholia', S.E., Vol. 14, p. 252.
[3] (1905d) *Three Essays on the Theory of Sexuality*, S.E., Vol. 7, p. 159 n2 (added 1924).

component in the sexual instinct. As we know, it can make itself independent and can, in the form of a perversion, dominate an individual's entire sexual activity. It also emerges as a predominant component instinct in one of the "pregenital organizations", as I have named them. But how can the sadistic instinct, whose aim it is to injure the object, be derived from Eros, the preserver of life? Is it not plausible to suppose that this sadism is in fact a death instinct which, under the influence of the narcissistic libido, has been forced away from the ego and has consequently only emerged in relation to the object? It now enters the service of the sexual function. During the oral stage of organization of the libido, the act of obtaining erotic mastery over an object coincides with that object's destruction; later, the sadistic instinct separates off, and finally, at the stage of genital primacy, it takes on, for the purposes of reproduction, the function of overpowering the sexual object to the extent necessary for carrying out the sexual act. It might indeed be said that the sadism which has been forced out of the ego has pointed the way for the libidinal components of the sexual instinct, and that these follow after it to the object. Wherever the original sadism has undergone no mitigation or intermixture, we find the familiar ambivalence of love and hate in erotic life.'[1]

The following most important proposition was put forward by Freud and rounds up his final views on the matter. 'It is our opinion, then, that in sadism and in masochism we have before us two excellent examples of a mixture of the two classes of instinct, of Eros and aggressiveness; and we proceed to the hypothesis that this relation is a model one—that every instinctual impulse that we can examine consists of similar fusions or alloys of the two classes of instinct.'[2]

In 'The Economic Problem of Masochism' Freud examines in detail the question of the existence of a primary masochism, but this in turn necessitates examining the question of sadism as well. 'The libido has the task of making the destroying instinct innocuous, and it fulfils the task by diverting that instinct to a great extent outwards—soon with the help of a special organic system, the muscular apparatus—towards objects in the external world. The instinct is then called the destructive instinct, the instinct for mastery, or the will to power. A portion of the instinct is placed

---

[1] (1920g) *Beyond the Pleasure Principle*, S.E., Vol. 18, p. 53 n.
[2] (1933a) *New Introductory Lectures on Psycho-Analysis*, S.E., Vol. 22, p. 104.

directly in the service of the sexual function, where it has an important part to play. This is sadism proper.'[1]

'If one is prepared to overlook a little inexactitude, it may be said that the death instinct which is operative in the organism— primal sadism—is identical with masochism.'[2]

[1] (1924c) 'The Economic Problem of Masochism', S.E., Vol. 19, p. 163.
[2] ibid., p. 164.

BISEXUALITY

1. *Definition*

Bisexuality is a biological concept,[1] and 'psycho-analysis has a common basis with biology, in that it presupposes an original bisexuality in human beings (as in animals). But psychoanalysis cannot elucidate the intrinsic nature of what in conventional or in biological phraseology is termed "masculine" and "feminine": it simply takes over the two concepts and makes them the foundation of its work'.[2] In psychoanalysis, bisexuality—universally to be found in the innate constitution of every human being[3]—refers to the tendency of human beings to distribute their libido 'either in a manifest or a latent fashion, over objects of both sexes'.[4]

Evidence of the universality of bisexuality can be found both on a physical and on a mental level. With regard to the former, Freud maintains that 'a certain degree of anatomical hermaphroditism occurs normally', i.e. traces are found in every individual of the apparatus of the opposite sex.[5] On a mental level, bisexuality manifests itself in a 'masculine or feminine attitude', neither of which are found in pure form in any individual,[6] but show them-

[1] (1950a [1887–1902]) *The Origins of Psycho-Analysis*, S.E., Vol. 1, p. 326 f; cf. different and more accurate translation of passage in S.E., Vol. 7, p. 4; (1905d) *Three Essays on Sexuality*, Vol. 7, p. 141; (1905e) 'Fragment of an Analysis of a Case of Hysteria', S.E., Vol. 7, p. 113 f.; (1910c) *Leonardo da Vinci*, S.E., Vol. 11, p. 136; (1940a [1938]) *An Outline of Psycho-Analysis*, S.E., Vol. 23, p. 188.

[2] (1920a) 'The Psychogenesis of a Case of Female Homosexuality', S.E., Vol. 18, p. 171; (1933a) *New Introductory Lectures on Psycho-Analysis*, S.E., Vol. 22, p. 114.

[3] (1950a [1887–1902]) *The Origins of Psycho-Analysis*, S.E., Vol. 1, p. 179; (1920a) 'The Psychogenesis of a Case of Female Homosexuality', S.E., Vol. 18, p. 156 n; (1923b) *The Ego and the Id*, S.E., Vol. 19, p. 31; (1925d) *An Autobiographical Study*, S.E., Vol. 20, p. 36; (1925j) 'Some Psychological Consequences of the Anatomical Distinction Between the Sexes', S.E., Vol. 19, p. 258; (1928b) 'Dostoevsky and Parricide', S.E., Vol. 21, p. 183 n; (1930a) *Civilization and its Discontents*, S.E., Vol. 21, p. 105 n.; n3; (1931b) 'Female Sexuality', S.E. Vol. 21, p. 227 f.

[4] (1937c) 'Analysis Terminable and Interminable', S.E., Vol. 23, p. 244.

[5] (1905d) *Three Essays on the Theory of Sexuality*, S.E., Vol. 7, p. 141; (1920a) 'The Psychogenesis of a Case of Female Homosexuality', S.E., Vol. 18, p. 170; (1933a) *New Introductory Lectures on Psycho-Analysis*, S.E., Vol. 22, p. 114.

[6] (1905d) *Three Essays on the Theory of Sexuality*, S.E., Vol. 7, p. 219 n, (added 1915); (1920a) 'The Psychogenesis of a Case of Female Homosexuality', S.E., Vol. 18, p. 170; (1925j) 'Some Psychological Consequences of the Anatomical Distinction Between the Sexes', S.E. Vol. 19, p. 258.

selves in the reactions of human beings which are all 'made up of masculine and feminine traits',[1] and in a mixture of character-traits belonging to both sexes.[2]

2. *Historical Development*

Freud took over the idea of a constitutional bisexuality from Fliess in the 1890s and soon recognized the important contribution which this concept could make to the understanding of the neuroses.[3] Around the turn of the century Freud even intended to write a book on 'bisexuality in man'.[4] Freud's views and formulations with regard to bisexuality remained consistent throughout his writings, with one important exception. Both Freud and Fliess originally held bisexuality 'responsible for the inclination to repression'.[5] In 1901 Freud still maintained that repression 'is only possible through reaction between two sexual impulses'[6] and that repression presupposes bisexuality;[7] furthermore, in 1905, he held the bisexual constitution responsible for the existence of the pair of opposites formed by sadism and masochism.[8] But in 1914 Freud explicitly repudiated the general validity of his Fliess' original hypothesis: 'To insist that bisexuality is the motive force leading to repression is to take too narrow a view'. At the same time he stated clearly that in many instances it is the ego which puts the repression into operation, 'for the benefit of one of the sexual tendencies'.[9]

Although Freud considered the concept of bisexuality as one of the clinical postulates of psychoanalysis,[10] he wrote as late as 1930 that the 'theory of bisexuality is still surrounded by many obscurities' and felt it as a particular impediment that no link with the theory of instincts had been found.[11] In his subsequent writings he

[1] (1925j) 'Some Psychological Consequences of the Anatomical Distinction Between the Sexes', S.E., Vol. 19, p. 255.

[2] (1905d) *Three Essays on the Theory of Sexuality*, S.E., Vol. 7, p. 219 n, (added 1915).

[3] (1950a [1887–1902]) *The Origins of Psycho-Analysis*, S.E., Vol. 1, p. 38.

[4] ibid., p. 334 n.   [5] ibid., p. 242.   [6] ibid., p. 334 f.

[7] ibid., p. 337.

[8] (1905d) *Three Essays on the Theory of Sexuality*, S.E., Vol. 7, p. 160.

[9] (1918b) 'From the History of an Infantile Neurosis', S.E., Vol. 17, p. 110; (1919e) 'A Child is Being Beaten', S.E., Vol. 17, pp. 200–2; (1937c) 'Analysis Terminable and Interminable', S.E., Vol. 23, p. 250. n.

[10] (1913j) 'The Claims of Psycho-Analysis to Scientific Interest', S.E., Vol. 13, p. 182.

[11] (1930a) *Civilization and its Discontents*, S.E., Vol. 21, p. 105 f., n3.

threw no new light on these obscurities, nor did he establish the missing link.

3. Bisexuality and the Libido Theory

The concept of bisexuality played an important part in the development of Freud's libido theory. Already in a letter to Fliess he had written that he was accustoming himself 'to the idea of regarding every sexual act as a process in which four persons are involved'.[1] He stated that a person's sexual constitution is derived from his initial bisexuality,[2] and that normal sexual manifestations cannot be understood without taking bisexuality into account.[3] 'In all of us, throughout life, the libido normally oscillates between male and female objects.'[4] He considered bisexuality as an important aetiological precondition of neuroses whose precipitating causes he saw in external 'frustrations and internal conflicts: conflicts between the three major psychical agencies, conflicts arising within the libidinal economy in consequence of our bisexual disposition and conflicts between the erotic and the aggressive instinctual components'.[5] Bisexuality comes to the fore much more clearly in women because they have two leading sexual organs, namely the clitoris and the vagina, which divide their sexual life into two phases. The first of these has a masculine character (clitoridal sexuality, masturbation) and only the second is specifically feminine. There is nothing analogous to such a diphasic sexual development in the man as he has only one leading sexual zone.[6]

4. Bisexuality and Dreams

Freud accepts the fact that 'the tendency of dreams and of unconscious phantasies to employ sexual symbols bisexually betrays an archaic characteristic. . . . But it is possible, too, to be misled into wrongly supposing that a sexual symbol is bisexual, if one forgets that in some dreams there is a general inversion of sex, so

---

[1] (1950a [1887–1902]) *The Origins of Psycho-Analysis*, S.E., Vol. 1, p. 289.

[2] (1900a) *The Interpretation of Dreams*, S.E., Vol. 5, p. 605 n.

[3] (1905d) *Three Essays on the Theory of Sexuality*, S.E., Vol. 7, p. 219 n.

[4] (1920a) 'The Psychogenesis of a Case of Female Homosexuality', S.E., Vol. 18, p. 158.

[5] (1931a) 'Libidinal Types', S.E., Vol. 21, p. 220.

[6] (1925j) 'Some Psychological Consequences of the Anatomical Distinction Between the Sexes', S.E., Vol. 19, p. 255; (1931b) 'Female Sexuality', S.E., Vol. 21, p. 227 n.

that what is male is represented as female and *vice versa*'.[1] In a 1911
addition to *The Interpretation of Dreams*, Freud states that 'we can
assert of many dreams . . . that they are bisexual, since they
unquestionably admit of an "over-interpretation" in which the
dreamer's homosexual impulses are realized—impulses, that is,
which are contrary to his normal sexual activities. To maintain,
however, as do Stekel . . . and Adler . . . that *all* dreams are to
be interpreted bisexually appears to me to be a generalization
which is equally undemonstrable and unplausible and which I am
not prepared to support'.[2]

5. *Bisexuality and the Oedipus Complex.* (*See Also Concept on the
Oedipus Complex*)
Freud put great emphasis on the importance of bisexuality with
regard to the oedipus complex. (a) It determines the outcome of the
oedipal situation: 'In both sexes the relative strength of the masculine and feminine sexual dispositions is what determines whether
the outcome of the oedipus situation shall be an identification with
the father or with the mother. This is one of the ways in which
bisexuality takes a hand in the subsequent vicissitudes of the
oedipus complex.'[3] (b) It is responsible for the more complete
(positive and negative) oedipus complex: 'the simple Oedipus
complex is by no means its commonest form. . . . Closer study
usually discloses the more complete Oedipus complex, which is
twofold, positive and negative, and is due to the bisexuality originally present in children: that is to say, a boy has not merely an
ambivalent attitude towards his father and an affectionate object-
choice towards his mother, but at the same time he also behaves
like a girl and displays an affectionate feminine attitude to his
father and a corresponding jealousy and hostility towards his
mother. It is this complicating element introduced by bisexuality
that makes it so difficult to obtain a clear view of the facts in connection with the earliest object-choices and identifications. . . .
It may even be that the ambivalence displayed in the relations to
the parents should be attributed entirely to bisexuality and that it

[1] [1911] [1925] (1900a) *The Interpretation of Dreams*, S.E., Vol. 5, p. 359,
(added 1911 and 1925).
[2] [1911] ibid., p. 396.
[3] (1923b) *The Ego and the Id*, S.E., Vol. 19, p. 33.

is not . . . developed out of identification in consequence of rivalry'.[1] (c) At the dissolution of the oedipus complex, bisexuality determines the relative strength of the identifications: 'At the dissolution of the oedipus complex the four trends of which it consists will group themselves in such a way as to produce a father-identification and a mother-identification. . . . The relative intensity of the two identifications in any individual will reflect the preponderance in him of one or the other of the two sexual dispositions.'[2]

6. *Bisexuality and Neurosis*

A 'strong innate bisexual disposition becomes one of the preconditions or reinforcements of neurosis',[3] and the strength of such a disposition is 'especially clearly visible in the analysis of psychoneurotics'.[4] The revival of repressed sexual impulses from infancy during later developmental periods may ultimately be due to our initial bisexuality, and they are 'able to furnish the motive force for the formation of psychoneurotic symptoms of every kind'.[5] Freud saw bisexuality as one of the organic bases of hysterical symptoms[6] and he postulated a 'bisexual nature of hysterical symptoms' in so far as they are the expression of both a masculine and a feminine unconscious fantasy. He did not, however, claim general validity for this formula.[7] But he emphasized the importance of realizing that a symptom may have a bisexual meaning so that it may 'persist undiminished although we have already resolved one of its sexual meanings'.[8] Jealousy, for instance, can be intensified and become neurotic if it is experienced bisexually, i.e. when a man does 'not only feel pain about the woman he loves and hatred of the man who is his rival, but also grief about the man,

[1] (1923b) *The Ego and the Id*, S.E., Vol. 19, p. 33; (1925d) *An Autobiographical Study*, S.E., Vol. 20, p. 36; (1925j) 'Some Psychological Consequences of the Anatomical Distinction Between the Sexes', S.E., Vol. 19, p. 249 n.

[2] (1923b) *The Ego and the Id*, S.E., Vol. 19, p. 34.

[3] (1928b) 'Dostoevsky and Parricide', S.E., Vol. 21, p. 184.

[4] (1908a) 'Hysterical Phantasies and their Relation to Bisexuality', S.E., Vol. 9, p. 165 n.

[5] (1900a) *The Interpretation of Dreams*, S.E., Vol. 5, p. 605 n.

[6] (1905e) 'Fragment of an Analysis of a Case of Hysteria', S.E., Vol. 7, p. 113 n.

[7] (1908a) 'Hysterical Phantasies and their Relation to Bisexuality', S.E., Vol. 9, pp. 164–6.

[8] ibid., p. 166.

whom he loves unconsciously, and hatred of the woman as his rival'.[1]

7. Bisexuality and Perversion

Inversion cannot be explained as psychical hermaphroditism, i.e. it is on the whole independent of somatic hermaphroditism. However, Freud held the view that 'a bisexual disposition is somehow concerned in inversion' and affects the 'sexual instinct in the course of development'.[2] The sexual object of an invert is someone who 'combines the characters of both sexes'[3] and is thus 'a kind of reflection of the subject's own bisexual nature'.[4]

8. Bisexuality and Conflict

In 'Analysis Terminable and Interminable' (1937) Freud deals with the problem why the majority of human beings cannot choose objects of either sex without interference of one trend with the other, in spite of the universality of our bisexual constitution. 'It is not clear why the rivals do not always divide up the available quota of libido between them according to their relative strength', unless one assumes an 'independently emerging tendency to conflict' which is due to 'the intervention of an element of free aggressiveness'.[5]

[1] (1922b) 'Some Neurotic Mechanisms in Jealousy, Paranoia and Homosexuality', S.E., Vol. 18, p. 223.
[2] (1925d) An Autobiographical Study, S.E., Vol. 20, p. 38.
[3] (1905d) Three Essays on the Theory of Sexuality, S.E., Vol. 7, p. 144.
[4] [1915], ibid., p. 144.
[5] (1937c) 'Analysis Terminable and Interminable', S.E., Vol. 23, p. 244.

INDEX

frustration, 76
fusion, concept of, 43, 72, 80–91; of
Eros and death instinct, 70, 75,
120

genital phase, 35–6
genital zone, 56; primacy of, 50, 53,
58, 64, 66, 98, 120
genitals, erotogenic zones attain significance of, 60
girl's psychological development, 95–6,
98
group formation, 78
guilt, 76, 89, 114

Hartmann, H.:
'The Development of the Ego Concept in Freud's Work', 16n.;
'Notes on the Theory of Sublimation', 88; with Kris. E., and
Loewenstein, R. M., 'The Function of Theory in Psychoanalysis',
15&n., 16n.
hate:
connected with ego instincts, 40;
as ego's reaction to external world,
74; and love, *see* love
hermaphroditism, physical, 105, 122,
127
homosexuality, 36, 103, 104–5, 110,
127